1 2   1 4

BOONE COUNTY LIBRARY

31010000414260

# GARDEN FLOWER
# FOLKLORE

WITHDRAWN

"A fascinating history."
—*Chicago Sun Times*

"Even if you're not an avid gardener, this book is entertaining reading."
—*Minneapolis Star-Tribune*

"Fascinating facts and folklore will enchant the reader, as will beautiful pen-and-ink illustrations."
—*Country Accents*

"Highly recommended."
—*Journal-Constitution*, Atlanta

Martin, Laura C.
Garden Flower Folklore

398.2,MAR

RSN=94037395     LOC=nabo

12  14  94   PO

Property of
North Arkansas Regional Library
Harrison, Arkansas

DEMCO

# GARDEN FLOWER FOLKLORE

## Laura C. Martin
### illustrations by Mauro Magellan
### color illustrations by Sharon Coogle

Property of
North Arkansas Regional Library
Harrison, Arkansas

The
Globe
Pequot
Press

**Old Saybrook, Connecticut**

Text and illustrations copyright © 1987 by Laura C. Martin

All rights reserved. No part of this book may be reproduced or transmitted in any form by any means, electronic or mechanical, including photocopying and recording, or by any information storage and retrieval system, except as may be expressly permitted by the 1976 Copyright Act or in writing from the publisher. Requests for permission should be made in writing to The Globe Pequot Press, P.O. Box 833, Old Saybrook, Connecticut 06475.

The Globe Pequot Press and Laura C. Martin disclaim any and all liability resulting from the use of, preparation of, ingestion of, or contact with any plant discussed in this book.

Library of Congress Cataloging-in-Publication Data

Martin, Laura C.
    Garden flower folklore / by Laura C. Martin; illustrations
      by Mauro Magellan ; color illustrations by Sharon Coogle.
      p. cm
    Bibliography: p.
    Includes index.
    ISBN 0-87106-766-8    ISBN 1-56440-611-3 (pbk)
    1. Flowers—Folklore. 2. Flower gardening. I. Magellan,
    Mauro. II. Coogle, Sharon. III. Title.
GR780.M37   1987
398.2'42—dc19                 87-17394
                               CIP

Manufactured in the United States of America
First Edition/Second Printing

# Contents

To my parents

Ken & Lois Coogle

in gratitude
for giving me
both roots
and wings

# Preface

The flowers discussed in *Garden Flower Folklore* are arranged according to blooming season: early spring, late spring, summer, fall, and winter. Within each of these parts, the flowers are listed alphabetically by the common name most often used.

Although the major thrust of this book is the folklore (the legends, stories, and superstitions) connected with each garden flower, a brief description of each plant and basic growing instructions are also included. The family name, genus, and selected species (as well as hybrids and cultivars, when appropriate) are listed for each plant. The species, hybrids, and cultivars listed are those that are most popular or are of outstanding horticultural value.

Several aspects of flower folklore were of such interest that special sections explain these in greater detail. These include such topics as the language of flowers (Names and Meanings of Flowers), the doctrine of signatures (Garden Flowers for Food and Medicine), how to treat cut flowers and garden plants suitable for using as dyes (Flowers for the Home), and flowers particularly beloved during different times in history (Gardens in History).

# Introduction

I am sitting at my kitchen window, delighted with the scene in front of me. The plants in my back yard are in full bloom. Several varieties of narcissus vie for attention with a few late-blooming crocus blossoms. The dark blue of grape hyacinth modestly peeks out from under the dogwood tree. It is a scene of springtime splendor, of the earth making up for months of drab winter weather.

I am not a particularly neat gardener, for I lack that streak of perfectionism that causes gardens to take on a manicured look. My garden sometimes looks haphazard, and my plants respond in proportion to the amount of time and attention I give them. They survive my benign neglect and shine under my sporadic periods of lavish attention.

Whatever their condition, however, I love my flowers and take great delight in discovering their personalities. Each different flower has a unique history and hidden talents. Some, I know, are aristocrats and deserve my respect and admiration for their illustrious past. Some are little more than dressed-up weeds, but these, too, deserve my love and attention, for they have been with me for many years.

My garden is a melting pot where hybrids and heirlooms stand side by side, each contributing something special to the garden. Some offer a splash of color, others a bit of delicate texture, and even others a whiff of unforgettable perfume.

Nearly all the flowers we grow in our gardens have rich and varied personalities. Some, such as the foxglove, have been important for their medicinal value. Others, such as the iris, have become symbols of victories and reminders of important events in history.

Some flowers have been hybridized so extensively that they now look completely different from their original form. Other flowers have stubbornly resisted the efforts of plant breeders and proudly hold on to their original good looks.

A study of flowers through the ages is a study of the history of humanity. The characteristics of different ages are reflected by the use of flowers during these different periods. For example, the excessive use of roses during Roman times indicates the extravagance of that period. The popularity of the lily (thought to be the flower sacred to the Virgin Mary) during the Middle Ages is symbolic of the power of the Christian church at that time. The language of the flowers, an elaborate system that assigned meaning to the flowers, was a natural outgrowth of the mood of Victorian England.

Flowers are, as the prophet Mohammed suggested, food for the soul. They are not essential to our everyday existence, but they are a wonderful and constant reminder of the abundant generosity of the earth. There is no biological reason for a rose to be so achingly beautiful, or for lilacs to have such an incredibly sweet scent. The fact that flowers volunteer such exquisite beauty is the miracle of the garden.

Gardeners throughout the world share a common spirit. We recognize one another, not only by the dirt under the fingernails, but also by the spirit of love and respect for the living world manifest in each of us. To plant a seed and watch it grow into the perfection of a flower is an experience that never gets old.

*Garden Flower Folklore* is written in dedication to the beauty of our garden flowers and in respect to the gardeners who are their keepers. May we all learn from the peace and harmony of our gardens.

# Early Spring

COMMON NAME: **basket of gold**
GENUS: *Alyssum* (although this plant is generally listed in catalogs as *Alyssum saxatile*, it can also be listed in the genus *Aurinia*)
SPECIES, HYBRIDS, CULTIVARS: *A. saxatile* 'Citrinum'—pale yellow flowers. *A.s.* 'Compactum'—bright yellow flowers; shorter plants. *A.s.* 'Flora Plenum'—double form; bright yellow; each flower is like a miniature rose.
FAMILY: Cruciferae
BLOOMS: early spring
TYPE: perennial
DESCRIPTION: Basket of gold is characterized by masses of yellow flowers. This is a splendid plant to use in rock gardens or as an edging plant. It is also quite effective in hanging baskets or in containers.
CULTIVATION: *Alyssum* prefers slightly acidic, not-too-rich soil that is well drained. Plants should be set out in the spring or fall. Seeds can be sown outdoors in seedbeds in late May. They should bloom from seed in approximately six weeks. After the plant blooms, cut it back to about half its height to stimulate new growth.

––––––– ❁ –––––––

Basket of gold was brought to the United States from Crete in the early 1700s. The genus name, *Alyssum*, comes from two Greek words, *a*, meaning "without," and *lysson*, meaning "rage" or "madness." The plant was given this name because at one time it was used to cure hydrophobia and other mental disorders. Other common names include madwort, also alluding to its supposed medicinal powers, and gold dust, referring to its lovely yellow gold flowers. *A. maritimum* (also referred to as *Lobularia maritima*) originally grew by the sea, as indicated by the name. This species has a lovely honey scent and is wonderful to include in a seaside garden.

According to superstition, if you wear a sprig of basket of gold, it will prevent anyone from getting angry with you.

Much confusion persists about the genus name. Although the original genus was divided into several new groupings, species found within this genus can now be found either as *Lobularia* or *Aurinia*, as well as *Alyssum*.

Basket of gold makes a very good cut flower.

COMMON NAME: **glory of the snow**
GENUS: *Chionodoxa*
SPECIES, HYBRIDS, CULTIVARS:
*C. luciliae* 'Alba'—white. *C.l.*
'Gigantea'—large blue flowers, 2 inches
across. *C. sardensis*—small, intensely blue
flowers.
FAMILY: Liliaceae
BLOOMS: early spring
TYPE: perennial
DESCRIPTION: Beautiful star-shaped
flowers in blue or white bloom very early in
spring, sometimes even before snow is gone.
Used in mass plantings, these plants can be
spectacularly beautiful. Their neat, compact
growing habit makes them good for growing
in rock gardens.
CULTIVATION: Bulbs of glory of the
snow should be planted in early fall, 2 to 3
inches deep, in full sun or partial shade.
Plants may need dividing occasionally. It will
self-sow fairly readily.

The genus name has been translated exactly
to give us the common name. *Chion* means
"snow," and *doxa* means "glory." Its early
blooms often come while there is still snow
on the ground. The species was named for
Lucile Boissier, wife of a botanist from
Geneva, Edmond Boissier. Mrs. Boissier died
while accompanying her husband on a plant
exploration trip to Spain in 1849.

The bright blue of the blossoms
provides a welcome spot of color in a late
winter floral arrangement.

Discovered in 1842, glory of the snow
was found growing at a height of 7,000 feet
in mountain meadows of Turkey. Discoverers
called it the "most sumptuous display of
floral beauty." A native of Crete and Asia
Minor, it was introduced for cultivation in
1877.

COMMON NAME: **grape hyacinth**
GENUS: *Muscari*
SPECIES, HYBRIDS, CULTIVARS:
*M. armeniacum* 'Early Giant'—blue. *M.a.*
'Blue Spike'—up to 12-inch blossoms. *M.a.*
'White Beauty'—white.
*M. botryoides*—pure white.
FAMILY: Liliaceae
BLOOMS: early spring
TYPE: perennial
DESCRIPTION: Most grape hyacinths
grow 6 to 8 inches tall and produce spikes
full of round, almost closed blossoms. They
spread about 3 inches and have foliage that is
long, narrow and grasslike.
CULTIVATION: Grape hyacinths come
from small bulbs, which should be planted 3
inches deep and 3 inches apart. For best
effect the bulbs should be planted in
quantities. They are particularly effective
under trees or shrubs. Grape hyacinths do
equally well in full sun or partial shade. The
leaves should be left to die back naturally
after the flowers bloom.

Some species of the genus *Muscari* have a
sweet, musky scent, and this is the reason
for the name, for *Muscari* is from the Greek
word *moschos*, or "musk." Many gardeners
originally grew the plant for its scent and not
its beauty. The species name *botryoides* is
also from Greek and means "a bunch of
grapes." This, along with the plant's physical
resemblance to the hyacinth, gives us the
common name, grape hyacinth.

M. *botryoides* is also called the starch
hyacinth, for it smells like starch.

Grape hyacinths are native to southern
Europe, Northern Africa, and western Asia.
The small bulbs have been used extensively
in cooking. It has been suggested that, boiled
in vinegar (to reduce the bitterness), the
bulbs of *M. comosa* and *M. atlanticum* can
be made into very tasty pickles. Other
species are so bitter that they have earned
the name *Bulbus vomitorium*. The
first-century Greek physician Discorides
wrote, "of this wort it is said that it was
produced out of dragon's blood, on top of
mountains, in thick forests."

COMMON NAME:  **hyacinth**
GENUS:  *Hyacinthus*
SPECIES, HYBRIDS, CULTIVARS:
*H. orientalis* 'Amsterdam'—bright red to
pink. *H.o.* 'Anne Marie'—light pink. *H.o.*
'Carnegie'—creamy white. *H.o.* 'Delft
Blue'—blue.
FAMILY:  Liliaceae
BLOOMS:  early spring
TYPE:  perennial
DESCRIPTION:  Hyacinths are widely
used as a spring bulb. The top flower size is
7 to 7½ inches in circumference. The flower
spike is composed of neatly rounded mounds
of small blossoms. Flowers are available in
pink, white, cream, reddish pink, blue,
yellow, and violet blue.
CULTIVATION:  Good drainage is a
must for this plant, because the bulbs rot
easily if water stands on them. Bulbs should
be planted in the fall, 6 inches deep, 6 to 8
inches apart. Mulch them in the fall to
protect the tender spring growth from frost
damage. Bulbs should be planted in an area
that gets full sun or partial shade.

According to mythology, hyacinths originated
because of the wrath of Zephyr, god of the
wind. Apollo, king of all the gods, fell in
love with Hyacinthus, son of the king of
Sparta. One day as Apollo and Hyacinthus
were playing quoits (a game similar to today's
horseshoes), Apollo threw the metal ring and
Zephyr, jealous and enraged, caused the
wind to make the metal ring hit Hyacinthus
and kill him. Broken hearted, Apollo created
the hyacinth flower out of the blood of his
friend. Some even say that the petals look
like the Greek syllables ai ai, meaning "woe."

In the Victorian language of flowers
hyacinth means sport or play, and the blue
hyacinth is a symbol of sincerity.

The Greeks dedicated this plant to
Ceres, the goddess of agriculture. In ancient
Sparta, annual Hyacinthian feasts were held.
A Greek girl wore a crown made from
hyacinth blossoms when she assisted at her
brother's wedding.

Greeks used concoctions made from the
plants to treat dysentery and the bite of
poisonous spiders. Such a concoction was
also reputed to have the power to prevent a
young boy's voice from changing during
puberty, making it very popular with singing
masters of the time.

Hyacinths were first found growing in
Asia Minor, as is suggested by the species
name *orientalis*. Cultivated in Turkey and
Persia, hyacinths were brought to England
from Persia in 1561.

The following story is told of how
hyacinths got to Holland: Trading ships
carrying crates of these exotic and expensive
bulbs wrecked off the coast of Holland. The
crates broke open, and the waves washed the
bulbs ashore, where they rooted and
produced beautiful flowers. However
hyacinths got to them, the Dutch lent their
magical hands to the plant, and by 1725
more than 2,000 varieties of hyacinth were
found in Europe. Though interest in the
bulbs never quite reached the level that tulips
created, the price of hyacinth bulbs was quite
high and competition for new varieties
fierce.

COMMON NAME: **pansy**
GENUS: *Viola*
SPECIES, HYBRIDS, CULTIVARS:
*V. wittrockiana* 'Universal' hybrids—
heavy blooms; heat and cold tolerant.
*V.w.* 'Crystal Bowl'—clear colors without
markings; small 2¹/₂-inch blooms.
*V.w.* 'Majestic Giants'—large plants with
4-inch blooms.
FAMILY: Violaceae
BLOOMS: early spring
TYPE: annual
DESCRIPTION: Unusual markings on
the petals of pansy blossoms have earned the
flowers the name "faces." There are many
flowers to each plant, each one borne on a
separate stem. Flowers come in many colors,
including blue, purple, yellow, apricot,
orange, mahogany, red, white, and bicolors.
CULTIVATION: In regions with a mild
climate, sow pansy seeds in late summer or
set out plants in early fall. In colder areas,
sow seeds indoors during January or
February and set out the plants in early
spring. Pansies like cool, moist soil that is
rich in organic matter. They are heavy
feeders and should be treated to applications
of a general fertilizer every two to three
weeks during the active growing season.

Pansies are all descendants of the small
Johnny-jump-up, *Viola tricolor.* The pansy's
transition from the small wildflower to the
beautiful garden flower resulted from the
dedicated efforts of an English gardener
named Thompson and the generosity of his
employer, Lord Gambier, a British naval
commander. Thompson experimented with
Johnny-jump-up for thirty years and finally
arrived at flowers that retained the lively
charm of the small wildflower but also had
the size and beauty necessary to please even
the most discriminating gardener. The spur

that is characteristic to the Violet family was
lost, and the petals were large and flat.

The folklore of the pansy is rich and
diverse. Johnny-jump-up is just one of
dozens (some even say hundreds) of common
names. The faces created by the patterns on
the petals give rise to names like monkey
faces, peeping Tom, and three faces in a
hood. Its supposed magical powers in the
ways of love resulted in names such as
cull-me-to-you, tickle-my-fancy,
love-in-idleness, kiss-her-in-the-pantry, and
heartsease. The three petals were thought to
be representative of the Christian doctrine of
the Trinity, and thus the flower was
sometimes called herb trinity.

According to German and Scottish
folktales, pansies were called stepmother:
The large lower petal is the mother, the two
large petals to either side of her are the
well-dressed daughters, and the two small
upper petals are the poor stepdaughters.

In another German story, the pansy at
one time had a wonderfully strong, sweet
scent. People would travel from miles around
to smell this scent. In doing so, however,
they would trample down the grasses
surrounding the pansy. Because this ruined
the feed for cattle, the pansy prayed to God
for help. God gave the plant great beauty but
took away the scent.

Pansies have always been associated
with love and thoughts of love. The Celts
made a tea from the dried leaves and used it
as a love potion. According to the doctrine
of signatures, pansy leaves, which are heart
shaped, were used to cure a broken heart.
Nicholas Culpeper, a seventeenth-century
English writer, said that a syrup made from
the flowers was used as a cure for venereal
disease.

Both the leaves and flowers are edible
and are high in vitamins A and C. The
flowers impart a strong flavor and have been
used to make syrup, flavor honey, and make
custard. Both the leaves and flowers can be

used as a garnish, such as on cold fruit or cream soups. The flowers are also useful as a dye.

The name pansy comes from the French word *pensèe*, which means "thought." This name was given many centuries ago, for the French believed that pansies could make your lover think of you. The three colors of the original pansy—purple, white, and yellow—were thought to symbolize memories, loving thoughts, and souvenirs. These were all things that ease the hearts of separated lovers.

Legend says that at one time all pansies were white, and it was not until they were pierced by cupid's arrow that they gained the purple and yellow colors. With the colors, however, came the magic power to be used in love potions. Shakespeare described the pansy as the flower that was ". . .before milk-white, now purple with love's wound."

Shakespeare was also well aware of the pansy's magic, which he used extensively in *A Midsummer-Night's Dream:*

*"The juice of it, on sleeping eye-lids laid,*
*Will make a man or woman madly dote*
*Upon the next live creature that it sees."*

The confusion arising from the power of the pansy in this play should convince anyone to use care when handling a love potion containing pansies.

Not all folktales about pansies have such pleasant connotations. According to English superstition, to pick a pansy with dew still on it will cause the death of a loved one.

Neil Ewart in *The Lore of Flowers* says that pansies were fortune tellers for the Knights of the Round Table. Plucking a pansy petal, the knights would look for secret signs. If the petal had four lines, this meant hope. If the lines were thick and leaned toward the left, this meant a life of trouble. Lines leaning toward the right signified prosperity until the end. Seven lines meant constancy in love (and if the center streak were the longest, Sunday would be the wedding day). Eight streaks meant fickleness, nine meant a changing of heart, and eleven signified disappointment in love and an early grave.

Peter Coats, a noted English garden writer, suggests another game to play with pansy petals: There were five girls who went to see their grandmother (pick off petals one by one) who was sick in bed (reveal little pouch, which looks like granny in bed with the sheets pulled up). "Grandma, you look so much better!" said the girls. "Thank you," said the grandmother, "but just look how thin my legs are" (remove the spur and pull out two skinny stamens).

According to the Victorian language of flowers, pansy means "to think" — particularly of love. It is, however, considered a bad-luck gift for a man.

COMMON NAME: scilla
GENUS: *Scilla*
SPECIES: *S. sibirica*
FAMILY: Liliaceae
BLOOMS: early spring
TYPE: perennial
DESCRIPTION: Scilla has short (4 to 6 inches) spikes of bright blue or white flowers. The foliage is attractive and the growing habit neat, making it an excellent plant to use as a border or edging plant. It also lends itself well to an informal setting and looks very good naturalized under trees or shrubs.
CULTIVATION: The small bulbs should be planted 4 inches deep in early fall. Give them an open, sunny spot, and they will multiply rapidly.

The Welsh name for this plant is cuckoo's boots. *S. bifolia* was described by John Gerard, author of a sixteenth-century herbal, as "small blew flowers consisting of sixe little leaves spread abrode like a star. The seed is contained in small round bullets."

During Elizabethan times, starch used for stiffening collars was made from the bulbs of this plant.

———— ❈ ————

Ten species of *Scilla* are native to Europe, and several of these have been cultivated for many centuries. Some records indicate that at least five species of *Scilla* were being cultivated as early as 1597.

The genus name means "I injure" and refers to the poisonous properties of the plant. Red scilla was even used as rat poison.

*Scilla* is often called squill. The bulbs of both the red and white squills were made into a concoction called a "syrup of squills." This supposedly had medicinal properties, and a drug found within the bulbs was used as a component in heart tonics. The physiological effects of eating this bulb were thought to be similar to those of inhaling tobacco, for both act on the nervous system. A Roman statesman suggested *Scilla* as a diuretic. It was also used to treat asthma and dropsy.

COMMON NAME:  sweet pea
GENUS:  *Lathyrus*
SPECIES:  *L. odoratus* (annual).
*L. latifolius* (perennial).
FAMILY:  Leguminosae
BLOOMS:  early spring
TYPE:  annual or perennial
DESCRIPTION:  The pastel blossoms of sweet peas come in a lovely array of hues including nearly every color except yellow. Their growth habit varies from creeping to bushy, and their height varies accordingly from 1 to 5 feet. Dainty and fragrant, sweet peas are a welcome sight in spring.
CULTIVATION:  Annual varieties of sweet peas will bloom best if given well-drained soil rich in humus, full sun, and regular watering. Plant seeds in very early spring, as soon as the ground can be worked, for spring blooms. For a climbing type, be sure to supply a trellis or other means of support. Perennial sweet peas are not nearly as exacting in their cultural needs and will survive quite well in average soils with moderate watering.

Plant hybridizers have worked virtual wonders on the original 6-foot-tall, weak-stemmed, small-flowered, but wonderfully fragrant sweet pea. Originally found growing in fields in Sicily, sweet peas adapted well to growing conditions in England, and by 1722 sweet peas were grown extensively there for their sweet fragrance. By the late 1800s breeders had created many different varieties of sweet peas, adding beauty to the sweet scent. Their popularity as a garden plant increased dramatically. They were especially popular during the late nineteenth century, and some people consider sweet peas the floral emblem for Edwardian England.

Sweet pea was used extensively as a cut flower and was an important part of flower arrangements at every dinner party and wedding. It was also used in corsages, nosegays, tussie-mussies, and boutonnieres. In the language of flowers, sweet pea meant departure or adieu. The dried petals were an important ingredient in potpourris.

Sweet pea fever reached a peak in England with the Bi-Centennial Sweet Pea Exhibition in 1900, when more than 250 varieties of sweet pea were displayed at the Crystal Palace in Sydenham. Praise for these delicate, sweet-scented flowers could not be high enough during the bicentennial. The Reverend W. T. Hutchins was reported saying that the sweet pea has "a fragrence like the universal gospel, yea, a sweet prophecy of welcome everywhere that has been abundantly fulfilled." In 1901 the English National Sweet Pea Society was formed.

Superstition holds that if you sow seeds of sweet pea before sunrise on Saint Patrick's Day (March 17), you will have blossoms that are larger and more fragrant. Some folks say that sowing them anytime between the feasts of Saints David and Chad (occurring on March 1 and 2) and of Saint Benedict (March 21) will give the same results.

The role of sweet pea in the study of heredity should not be overlooked, for it was on this plant that Father Gregor Mendel first performed his famous work in genetics.

Sweet pea is often considered the flower for April.

The genus name *Lathyrus* comes from the Greek word for pulse.

# Late Spring

COMMON NAME: ajuga
GENUS: *Ajuga*
SPECIES, HYBRIDS, CULTIVARS:
*A. pyramidalis*—10 inches tall with blue flowers; does not spread. *A. reptans* 'Alba'—spikes of white flowers grow only 6 inches tall; foliage is dark green. *A.r.* 'Burgandy Glow'—creeps extensively; flowers are blue; foliage has unusual coloration—new growth is bright burgandy, older leaf growth is creamy white and dark pink.
FAMILY: Labiatae
BLOOMS: late spring
TYPE: perennial
DESCRIPTION: This low-growing, mat-forming plant makes a wonderful ground cover. Many different species are available, several of which are used extensively in Europe. In mild climates the foliage is evergreen, and it forms such dense mats that weeds cannot grow through.
CULTIVATION: Ajuga needs to grow in sun or light shade. It spreads very quickly. For fast, good coverage, space plants 6 inches apart. Divide the plants in early spring or fall.

The genus name *Ajuga* means "not yoked" and was given to this plant because the sepals surrounding the bud are not connected. The species *reptans* describes the creeping growth habit characteristic of the plant.

There is some controversy as to the medicinal value of ajuga, or bugleweed, as it is sometimes called. Some say that he who has the bugleweed has no need of a surgeon. This alludes to its ability to stop bleeding—the sap contains tannin, a styptic. Because of this characteristic, the plant is also sometimes called carpenter's-herb, suggesting that not-too-precise carpenters who sometimes hit their thumbs might find good use for this plant.

Other common names include middle comfrey, common bugle, and sicklewort.

Ajuga can be used as a black dye for wool.

COMMON NAME: **bellflower**

GENUS: *Campanula*

SPECIES, HYBRIDS, CULTIVARS:
*C. glomerata* 'Joan Elliott'—clustered
bellflower; deep violet-blue; May-June. *C.*
*medium* 'Caerulea'; blue. *C. rotundifolia*
'Olympica'—bluebell of Scotland; blue;
June-September; 12 inches. *C. carpatica*
'China Doll'—lavender blue; 8 inches. *C. c.*
'Wedgewood Blue'—5 to 6 inches. *C. c.*
'Wedgewood White'—white; 8 inches.

FAMILY: Campanulaceae

BLOOMS: late spring, summer

TYPE: biennial and perennial

DESCRIPTION: There are many kinds
of bellflowers. Most have cup-shaped flowers
and small leaves, and colors come in blue,
lavender, and white. Cultivars of *Campanula*
*carpatica* are perennials that grow only
about 8 inches tall and are used in mass
plantings in borders or in rock gardens.
These do not have the "saucer" part that is
present in the other species.

CULTIVATION: Different species have
distinctly different cultural requirements, so
positively identify species you want to grow
in your garden. Bellflowers can be grown in
full sun or partial shade, and they thrive in
average garden soil. Seeds can be sown in
June for blooms the following year. Sow
seeds 1/8 inch deep, and thin plants to 12
inches apart. Perennial plants should be
divided in fall or spring. Remove faded
blossoms to prolong flowering. The
Carpathian bellflower, *C. carpatica*, should
spread nicely after a period of about three to
four years. This plant blooms well from June
until October. Canterbury bells, *C. medium*,
needs mulch in winter in cold climates.
These do best in full sun but will grow in
half-day or filtered sunlight as well.

———— ✿ ————

Bellflowers are known by a multitude of
common names. Some of the more colorful
ones are wild hyacinth, Venus looking glass,
Canterbury bells, our Lady's nightcap,
Mercury violet, viola mariana, mariets,
coventry bells, bats in the belfry, and our
Lady's thimble. Most of these, of course,
refer to the bell-shaped flower. The genus
name, *Campanula*, is from the Latin word
for little bell.

The name Venus looking glass comes
from a legend in which Venus, the goddess
of love and beauty, lost her magic mirror.
Anyone who looked in this mirror would see
nothing but beauty. A poor shepherd boy
found it, became entranced with his own
image, and did not want to give it back.
Venus sent Cupid down to get it back, and in
his haste, Cupid struck the shepherd's hand.
The mirror shattered, and everywhere a
piece of it landed, this flower began to grow.

*C. rapunculus* was made famous by the
brothers Grimm. In the story of Rapunzul a
man stole a piece of the bellflower from the
garden of a witch for his pregnant wife. The
witch caught him and made him promise
that when the child was born, she would be
given to the witch and named after the plant
he had stolen. This is how Rapunzul got her
name and inherited all her problems.

In addition to providing inspiration for
fairy tales, *C. rapunculus* has other
attributes. It is called the native English
rampion and has been cultivated since the
fifteenth century. It is supposedly an
excellent vegetable and can be eaten raw like
a radish. The roots are said to be sweet
because they store food in the form of sugar,
rather than starch. Leaves and blossoms of
this plant were made into concoctions used
to treat sore throats.

An old superstition about rampion is
that if you grow it in your garden, your
children will be quarrelsome.

Other names for species of bellflowers
suggest even more uses. Chimney bellflower
is grown in pots during summer months and
placed in empty fireplaces for decoration.

Still another bellflower species is called throatwort and was used as a gargle.

Be sure you know one species from another before you start munching on bellflowers, however, for the fresh bulbs of some species are considered poisonous.

Substances from these bulbs can be used as glue for book binders or as a substitute for starch.

Bellflower is the symbol of constancy and kindness.

COMMON NAME: **bleeding heart**
GENUS: *Dicentra*
SPECIES, HYBRIDS, CULTIVARS:
*D. eximia*—fringed bleeding heart; deep
red pink. *D. spectabilis*—bleeding heart;
30 inches tall; May-June. *D.s. 'Alba'*—white
bleeding heart; not as hardy as the pink.
FAMILY: Fumariaceae
BLOOMS: late spring
TYPE: perennial
DESCRIPTION: Exquisite heart-shaped
flowers are borne on gracefully arching
racemes. Different species range in height
from 18 inches *(eximia)* to 30 inches
*(spectabilis)*. The foliage is medium green,
finely dissected, and attractive.
CULTIVATION: Bleeding heart is
particularly welcomed by gardeners who
have a lot of shade, for the plants do best
without any direct sun. A shady, open spot is
ideal. The plants prefer soil rich in humus
and need ample moisture. Roots can be
divided in spring, or the plants can be
propagated by taking root cuttings in early
summer. If propagated from seed, bleeding
heart should be sown into flats in
midsummer.

About 150 species of bleeding heart can be
found in North America, western Asia, and
the Himalayas. The name *Dicentra* is from
two Greek words, *dis*, meaning "two," and
*kentros* meaning "spurs," and refers to the
unusual flower shape. The species name,
*spectabilis*, means "worthy of notice."

The common name, bleeding heart,
comes from a Chinese legend that said the
blossoms of the plant resembled a heart with
a drop of blood. Other common names for
this plant are Chinamen's breeches, lady's
locket, our Lady in a boat, and lyre flower.

In 1846 an English botanist, Robert
Fortune, returned from a plant exploration
trip to the Orient with the largest single
plant shipment ever to arrive in England. A
new type of terrarium developed to keep
plant specimens alive for an extended period
made the shipment possible. Among the
plants was a single bleeding heart collected
from the Grotto Gardens on the island of
Chusan. The plant was given to the Royal
Horticultural Society. It adapted quite well to
the English climate and propagated easily,
making it particularly popular with English
gardeners.

Although America has its own native
bleeding heart *(D. eximia)*, it is not as showy
as the cultivated variety. It also has the
decided disadvantage of causing dermatitis
upon contact with any of its parts.

As pioneers in America moved
westward, they moved out of shipping range
for the nurseries. Homesteaders still wanted
the ornamental plants that they had enjoyed
back East, and to fill this need plant peddlers
came into being. These individuals, the most
famous of whom was Johnny Appleseed,
traveled from one area to another selling
seeds and plants. Bleeding heart was one
plant the plant peddlers could always count
on selling.

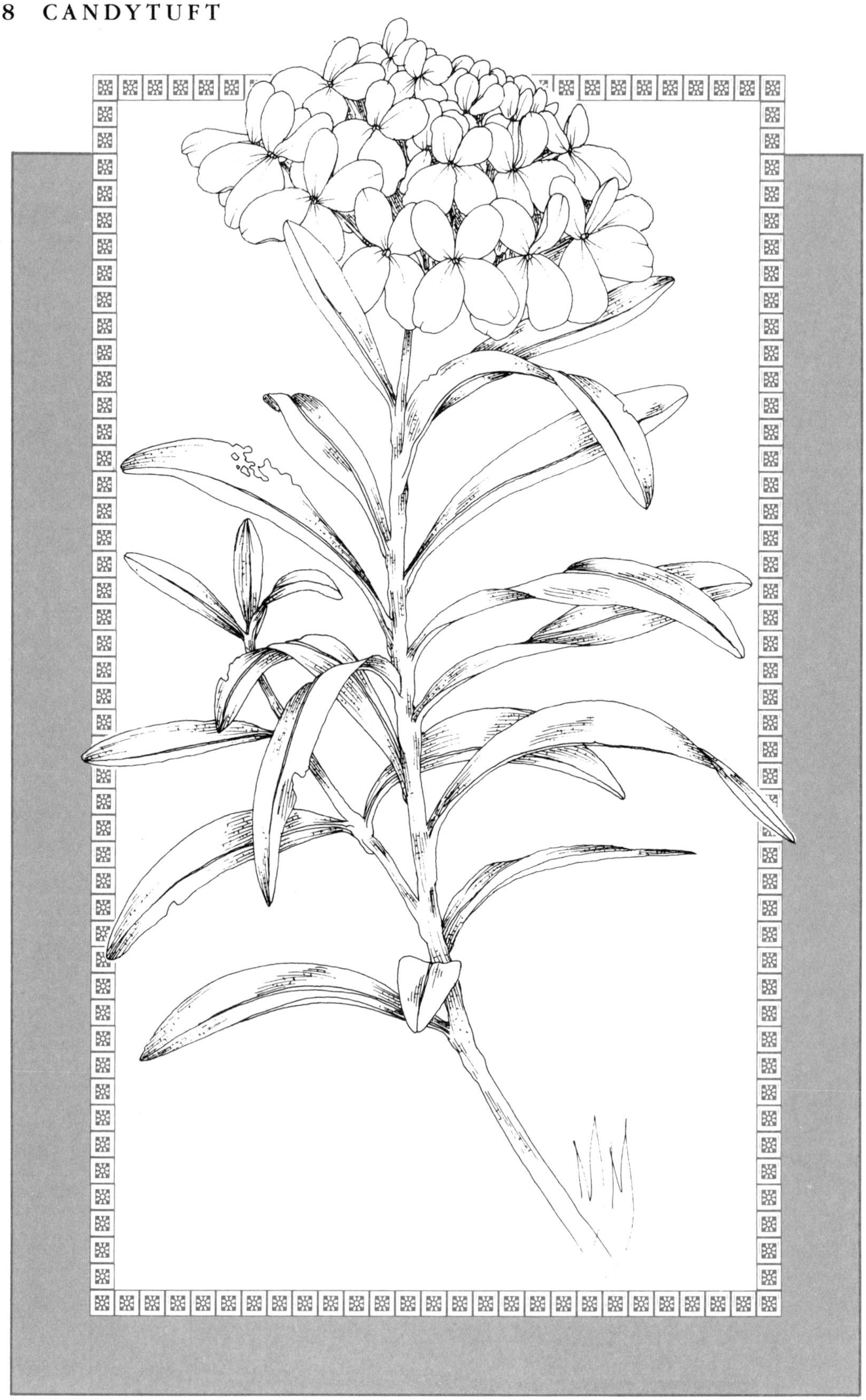

COMMON NAME:  candytuft
GENUS:  *Iberis*
SPECIES, HYBRIDS, CULTIVARS:
*I. sempervirens* 'Autumn Snow'—blooms
spring and fall; 9 inches. *I.s.* 'Purity'—7
inches. *I.s.* 'Pygmea'—4 inches. All the
preceeding are perennial forms. Annuals are
often found in pink and lavender tones: *I.
amara* and *I. umbellata.*
FAMILY:  Cruciferae
BLOOMS:  spring
TYPE:  Perennial and annual
DESCRIPTION:   Dark, evergreen leaves
and a shower of white spring flowers make
candytuft a nice addition to the perennial
bed in spring. The leaves might look a bit
ragged by late winter, but a little selective
pruning will go a long way toward creating a
lovely mass of blooms by late spring. Because
of its growth habit, candytuft is often called
a sub-shrub.
CULTIVATION:   Rich, well-drained
garden soil, ample moisture, and full sun are
necessary for growing candytuft. Annual
varieties can be grown from seeds sown
directly in the garden bed in late spring or
early summer. Perennial species can be
propagated by taking cuttings in late summer.

Candytuft, candyedge, or candyturf, as it
was sometimes called, was first found
growing on the shore of the Mediterranean
Sea. The name candy is from Candia, the
ancient name of Crete.

The genus name, *Iberis*, is from the
Roman name for ancient Spain, Iberia. Many
species of *Iberis* are native to Spain.

A member of the mustard family,
candytuft was often called candy mustard
and was used as a cheap substitute for
mustard. Although this was a very popular
practice among the common folk, the upper
class scorned this idea, and for many years
candytuft was rarely grown in estate gardens.

The perennial candytuft did not suffer
the effects of snobbery, for it is a
wonderfully beautiful plant, first sent to
Chelsea Gardens in London from Persia in
1793. According to the Oriental language of
flowers, perennial candytuft was a symbol of
indifference, because it is adaptable to a wide
range of conditions.

Candytuft was often used to treat
rheumatism and was at one time included in
almost every herb garden for this purpose.
An infusion made from all parts of the plant
was said to be particularly soothing.

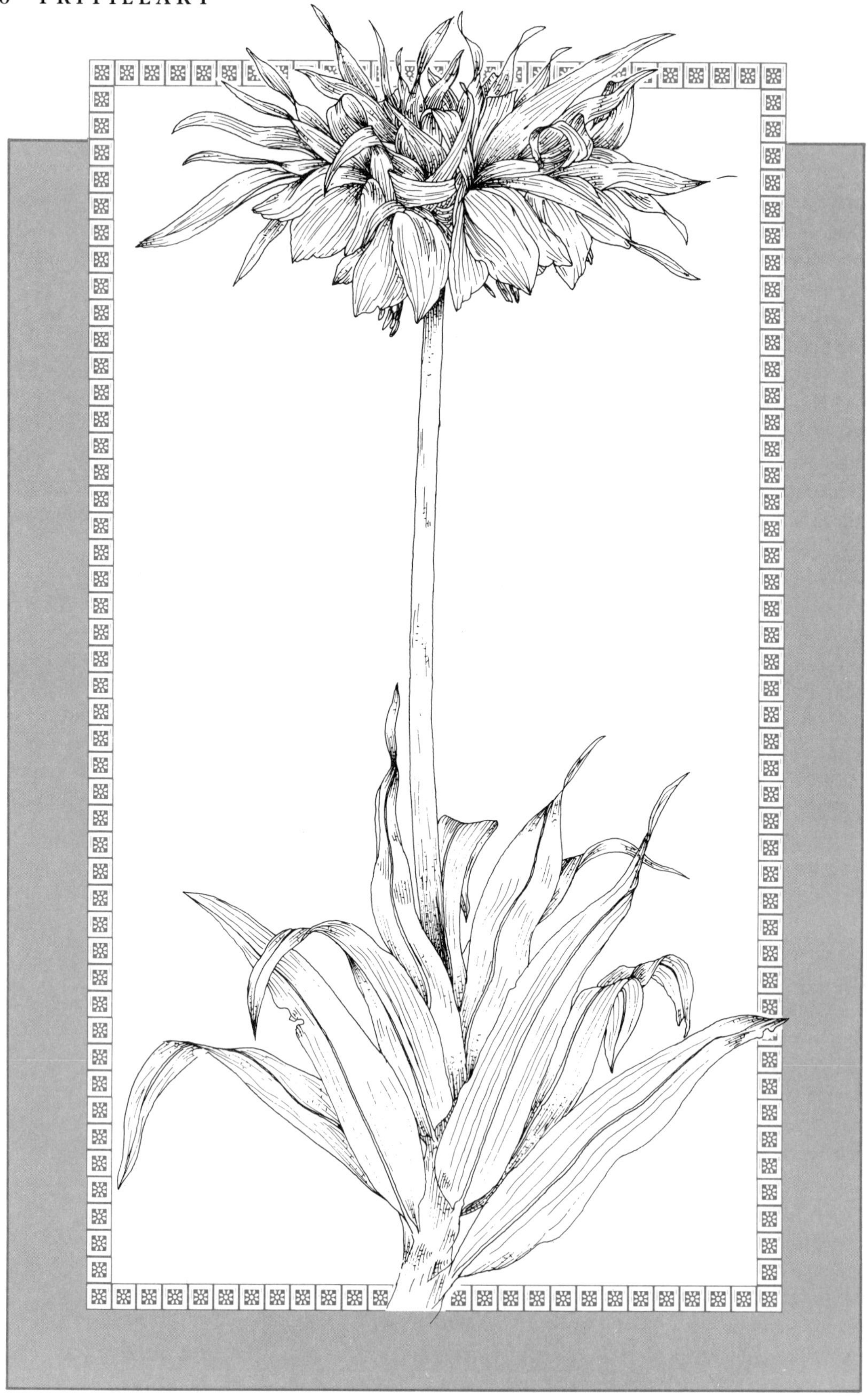

COMMON NAME: **fritillary**
GENUS: *Fritillaria*
SPECIES, HYBRIDS, CULTIVARS:
*F. imperialis*—large (3 feet); red or yellow.
*F. meleagris*—April; 12 inches; white or
checkered purple and maroon.
FAMILY: Liliaceae
BLOOMS: spring
TYPE: perennial
DESCRIPTION: The largest of the
fritillaries is the Crown Imperial *(F.
imperialis).* It has unusual large red or
yellow flowers (sometimes as many as eight
to ten to a stem) and grows to be 3 feet tall.
The blossoms are nodding and bell shaped,
the leaves long and narrow.
CULTIVATION: Fritillaries are
sometimes difficult to establish and are not
hardy in extremely northern regions. They
like well-drained, sandy soil and full sun or
partial shade. Plant the bulbs 8 inches deep
for *F. imperialis*, or 4 inches deep for *F.
meleagris*, in the fall. They may need lifting
and dividing every two to three years. Forget
trying to grow them from seed; it takes four
to six years to get blooms.

Fritillaries have many common names. Many
species are native to Persia (called Iran today)
and are thus called Persian lilies. Fritillary
was cultivated for many years in Turkey and
was brought to Europe, where it became
very popular. Often called Crown Imperial,
fritillary was said to have first bloomed in
Europe in the garden of an Austrian emperor.
By 1572 the plant was found blooming near
Orleans and was taken to England by the
Huguenots fleeing from France.

Londoners loved this large, unusual-
looking lily, and its popularity grew quickly.
Its unique appearance gave rise to many
common names. Sullen lady, drooping tulip,
and drooping young man all referred to the
fact that the flowers hang down. Toad's

head, snake flower, turkey eggs, and snake's
head fritillary allude to the unusual
appearance of the flower when in bud. The
checkered appearance of *F. meleagris* gave
rise to names like leopard lily, leper's lily,
Lazarus bell, guinea hen flower, and
checkered bell. The botanical names also
refer to the unusual shape and markings, for
the genus name is from the Latin word
*fritillus*, meaning ''a dice cup,'' and
*meleagris* means ''guinea hen,'' suggesting
that the blossoms resemble the speckled
feathers of the hen.

Rubbing the bulb produces a most
unpleasant odor, somewhat like a fox's den.
For this reason the flower is sometimes
called stink lily. This bulb is poisonous when
raw, though the Persians are said to have
eaten the bulbs after boiling them.

At the base of the blossoms there
generally lies a drop of nectar. Folktales and
superstitions have suggested that this is not
nectar, but a single tear drop. Stories of how
this tear appeared vary greatly from one
country to another. Persian folktales tell of a
beautiful queen who was unjustly accused by
her husband of being unfaithful. An angel
took pity on this poor lady and changed her
into this flower, but the flower, too, will cry
until the queen and her husband are reunited
in love.

According to another story the fritillary
holds tears within its blossoms because it
refused to bow its head when Christ passed
on Good Friday. Now the tears are there
forever and will not fall even in strong winds
or when shaken.

COMMON NAME:  **gazania**
GENUS:  *Gazania*
SPECIES, HYBRIDS, CULTIVARS:
hybrids developed from *G. rigens* and
*G. longiscapa*
FAMILY:  Compositae
BLOOMS:  late spring–summer
TYPE:  perennial (often grown as an
annual)
DESCRIPTION:   Gazania is
characterized by large, bright, daisylike
flowers. Blossom colors include shades of
yellows and reds, white, and cream. The
leaves have an unusual silvery cast and are
beautiful blowing in the breeze. Plants grow
to a height of only 6 to 8 inches. Flowers
generally measure 3 to 4 inches across.
CULTIVATION:   Gazania is very easy to
grow because it is so adaptable to a wide
range of conditions. It does not like the cold,
however, and should be treated as an annual
in areas that get frost. In these areas an easy
method of propagation is to take cuttings in
the fall and overwinter them indoors.
Gazania likes full sun and light, sandy soil.
Plants are drought tolerant and good to use
in hot, dry areas.

Gazanias produce two distinct types of
leaves: one is entire and narrow and the
other is deeply lobed. The flowers close up
at night and during cloudy weather. Gazania
does not make a good cut flower.

———— 🦎 ————

This genus was named for Theodore Gaza, a
Palestinian Greek scholar who translated
many ancient Greek writings into Latin
during the fifteenth century. There are
approximately forty species in this genus, all
of which are native to Africa.

One of the most successful hybrids was
developed from *G. rigens* and *G. splendens*.

The flowering period varies, depending
on the climate where gazania is grown. If
grown as an annual, it will bloom from late
spring until autumn. In frost-free areas it will
bloom all year long.

COMMON NAME: **gerber daisy**
GENUS: *Gerbera*
SPECIES: *G. jamesonii*
FAMILY: Compositae
BLOOMS: late spring-summer
TYPE: perennial
DESCRIPTION: Large, bright, daisylike flowers are borne on strong, 20- to 24-inch stems. Flowers measure 2 to 2½ inches across and can be single or double. Colors include white, yellow, red, and orange. The leaves are attractive, tongue-shaped, and lobed.
CULTIVATION: In southern areas this plant can be left in the ground over the winter if it is protected with mulch. In northern areas, pot it up in the fall and enjoy it indoors. Plant gerber daisy outdoors in full sun in moist, rich soil. Place the crowns slightly above ground level to keep them from rotting. Water this plant deeply and regularly, but allow the soil to dry slightly between watering. Fertilize it with liquid fertilizer.

Forty-five species of this genus are native to the hottest parts of Africa and Asia. Other common names for *G. jamesonii* include Transvaal daisy (from its original home, the Transvaal plain) and Barberton daisy.

The genus was named for a German naturalist, Traugott Gerber, who died in 1743. Another great German plant breeder, Robert Diem, specialized in gerber daisies and became famous for his beautiful specimens of this plant.

Gerber daisies come in many crayon colors and are outstanding because the petals are arranged in such perfect order. Many people think they look almost artificial, so evenly are the plant parts arranged. They make wonderful cut flowers, sometimes lasting as long as three weeks in water. They are economically very important to the flower trade in Holland.

Do not cut the blooms until they are fully opened. Once you bring the blossoms indoors, make sure that they stand upright in water. If they are allowed to lie horizontally for even a short time, the flower heads will droop and the stems will bend.

COMMON NAME:   **globe flower**
GENUS:   *Trollius*
SPECIES, HYBRIDS, CULTIVARS:
*T. asiaticus* 'Byrne's Giant'—lemon yellow;
24 to 30 inches. *T. cultorum* 'Prichard's
Giant'—large flowers; 30 inches.
*T. ledebourii*—orange flowers; 30 inches.
FAMILY:   Ranunculaceae
BLOOMS:   late spring
TYPE:   perennial
DESCRIPTION:   Globe flower has large
buttercup-shaped yellow or orange flowers,
usually measuring 2 inches across. The plant
grows 24 to 30 inches tall. The foliage is
dark green and finely dissected.
CULTIVATION:   Globe flower likes rich,
damp soil and partial shade. It is good to use
in a corner of the garden where the soil stays
too damp for many other plants. If it is given
sufficient moisture, globe flower can also be
grown in full sun.

Globe flower makes a very good cut flower,
the yellows blending well with blue of
forget-me-not or some of the bellflowers.
After the flowers have been cut, dip the
stems in boiling water for several seconds,
and then put the length of the stem in cool
water.

The genus name is from the German
word *trollblume*, meaning "globelike
flower," and refers to the multitude of lovely
buttercuplike sepals that surround the tiny,
insignificant petals, forming a round globe
shape.

A Scandinavian fairy tale says that trolls
would unlock the flowers at night, putting a
drop of poison in the cup. In this way they
hoped to trick the herdsmen and dairymaids
who would come to the fields the next day.

The Scottish name for globe flower is
*lucken gowan, lucken* meaning "closed" or
"shut up," and *gowan* or *gollande*, meaning
"flower."

The flowers are particularly fragrant
while drying, and in Sweden people would
strew them over the floor on holidays.

The yellow globe flower was
particularly abundant in England and was
often found growing near water mills, since
they thrived in the damp, rich ground found
there. The blossoms were often gathered
with much festivity during the month of
June and used to decorate churches and
cottages.

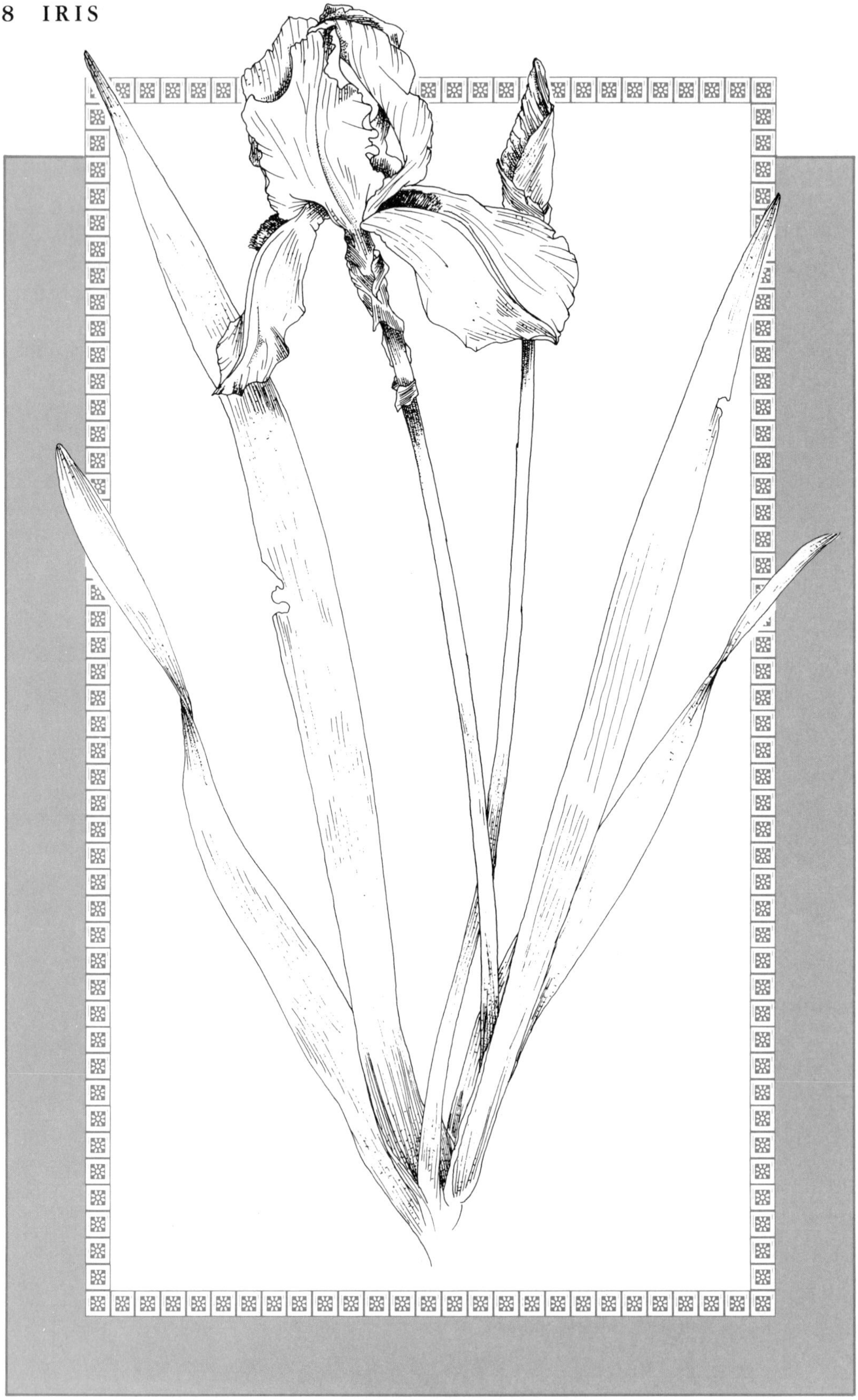

COMMON NAME: **iris**
GENUS: *Iris*
SPECIES, HYBRIDS, CULTIVARS:
There are over 200 known species of iris.
Some of the most popular garden irises
include (in order of succession of bloom): *I. reticulata*, Dutch, dwarf bearded,
intermediate bearded, tall bearded, Siberian,
Spuria, Louisiana, Japanese.
FAMILY: Iridaceae
BLOOMS: spring–summer
TYPE: perennial
DESCRIPTION: The bearded irises are
composed of standards (petals that stand
upright) and falls (petals that hang
downward). The beards are in the center of
the falls. Bearded irises are tall and stately,
bloom in May and June, and can be found in
nearly any color except clear red. The leaves
are flat, pointed, and sword shaped.

The beardless iris differs from the
bearded in that the petals are all more
horizontal, rather than up-and-down. It, of
course, lacks a beard, has smaller blossoms,
and has leaves that are narrow and almost
reedlike. There is much less color and size
variation among the beardless irises.
CULTIVATION: Bearded irises can
withstand long dry periods in the dormant
state but need abundant moisture when in
bloom. Rhizomes should be lifted and
divided every three to four years. Cultivate
the soil around the clumps and lightly
fertilize them in early spring. Fall chores
include cutting back the plant to within 4 to
5 inches of the rhizome and removing dead
or shriveled leaves. Watch irises closely
throughout the year for pest infestation and
treat them accordingly. Though they are
adaptable as to the type of soil, fertility is of
utmost importance, as is full sun.

Beardless, Japanese, Siberian, and
Spurian irises all need full sun. Louisiana iris
(a hybrid developed from several species
native to the southeastern United States)

thrives in sun or partial shade. Other
requirements are similar to those of the
bearded iris. Generally this group is more
adaptable and easier to grow than the
bearded types.

Iris is the sacred flower of the goddess of the
rainbow, Iris, who would take messages of
love from the "eye of heaven" to earth, using
the rainbow as a bridge. Iris means "eye of
heaven" and is the name given to the
goddess, this flower, and the center of your
own eye, meaning each of us carries a bit of
heaven with us. Because of its connection
with the goddess Iris, this plant is considered
the symbol of communication and message.
Greek men would often plant iris on the
graves of their beloved women as a tribute to
the goddess Iris, whose duty it was to take
the souls of women to the Elysian fields.

The iris has been an important emblem
for French people since the year A.D. 496
when Clovis I was fighting an important
battle and found himself trapped on one side
by the opposing army and the other side by
a broad river. Clovis's queen was a devout
Christian and had been begging him for
years, without success, to convert to
Christianity. When Clovis found himself
trapped, he prayed to the Christian god and
promised if he got out of this predicament
that he would convert and urge his followers
to do the same. As he finished the prayer,
according to the legend, Clovis looked out
across the river and saw a yellow flag iris
growing midway across. He realized that the
river must be shallow if the iris could grow
there. He took it as a sign from God and
marched his army across the shallow river to
victory. Keeping his promise, Clovis I and
3,000 of his followers converted to
Christianity on Christmas Day of that year.

The three large petals of iris represent faith, wisdom, and valor.

Charles IV (1294–1328) is thought to be the first ruler to include the iris on the French banner. It continued to appear from time to time on the French banner and is the basis for the French fleur-de-lis.

The oldest story about the iris is from 1479 B.C., when an Egyptian king, Thutmose III, returned home after conquering Syria. To commemorate his conquests he had pictures of irises and other flowers from his conquered lands drawn on the walls of a temple.

Throughout the ages iris has been used extensively as medicine and in cosmetics. The Romans, Egyptians, and Moors all grew it for its medicinal value and used it to treat such varied ailments as ague, epilepsy, chill and fever, headaches, loose teeth, and the bite of an adder. The iris root was so esteemed for its medicinal properties that the plant was grown in herb gardens throughout the Middle Ages. The roots, mixed with honey or wine, were supposed to be good for colds and coughs and "torments of the belly." It was also considered good for the bite of a venomous beast and for sunburn.

Not everyone could successfully harvest the iris roots, however; Pliny suggested that only those in a state of chastity could gather the roots.

In Germany the iris (or orrisroot, as it was called) was suspended in a barrel of beer to keep it from getting stale. The French used it to enhance the bouquet of wines. In Russia, iris root was used to flavor a soft drink made from honey and ginger. The ancient Greeks used iris in the manufacturing of perfume. It was used as a fixative because it strengthened other odors.

In Elizabethan England, strings of orrisroot were put into the laundry to sweetly scent the clothes.

Today the single greatest use of iris (other than for its beauty in the garden) is in the manufacturing of cosmetics. In Mexico, *I. florentina* is grown extensively for this purpose and many tons of the root are shipped to France annually.

Many species of iris produce a wonderful dye. Blossoms of the yellow flag iris *(I. pseudacorus)* make a good yellow dye, and the roots of this species make a good brown and black dye. The petals of purple iris, mixed with alum, make a beautiful blue-violet dye. To obtain the most potent color for dyes, the flowers should be gathered during a dry spell.

As a result of a wonderful legal loophole, irises can occasionally be found growing on roofs in Japan. This dates back to a time in Japan when the people were not allowed to grow any flower in their gardens that was not approved by the emperor. Irises were not on the approved list, so instead of growing them in their gardens, Japanese gardeners grew them on the roofs.

Iris is the state flower of Tennessee.

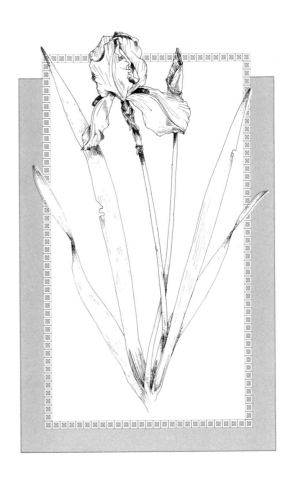

COMMON NAME: **lily**
GENUS: *Lilium*
SPECIES, HYBRIDS, CULTIVARS:
Many of the 200 species of lilies are native to the United States. Plant breeders have done extensive hybridization work on the lilies to make them hardy and free flowering. Lilies are now available in every color except blue.
FAMILY: Liliaceae
BLOOMS: late spring
TYPE: perennial
DESCRIPTION: Lilies are one of the most beautiful of all garden plants. The flowers are large and deliciously colored, and they usually occur many to a stem. The height of lilies ranges between 2 and 6 feet. Flower forms include trumpet shape, pendant, flat faced, or bowl shaped.
CULTIVATION: The most important requirement for growing lilies is well-drained soil. Water standing on the bulbs will cause them to rot. The bulbs should be kept cool. This can be done by overplanting with annuals or perennials. Depending on the size of the bulbs, they should be planted 4 to 8 inches deep in the fall. Lilies prefer soil that is slightly acidic and rich in organic matter. When planting, add a bit of bone meal mixed into the soil at the bottom of the hole. Any lily that grows more than 3 feet tall should be staked. Be sure to water lilies generously while they are in bloom and use a complete fertilizer in early spring as the stems emerge, again when the buds form, and after they have bloomed.

———— ❧ ————

According to the Victorian language of flowers, the lily is a symbol of majesty. Certainly the regal lily has always been beloved by both princes and paupers from all over the world. Greek and Roman mythologies mention the lily often, as do legends from China and Japan.

The tiger lily grows wild in Korea, where it was revered for both its beauty and its delicate flavor. It was considered a symbol of war. This lily was brought to Europe from the Orient in 1804 by plant collector William Kerr.

Lilies have been cultivated for over 5,000 years, since the Sumerian culture developed in the Tigris-Euphrates Valley. One Sumerian city was named Susa, another name for lily. Some scholars insist that the city was named for the flower; others suggest that it was the other way around.

The lily has often been associated with religious figures. It was thought to be sacred to the Minoan goddess Britomartis; was considered the flower of Saint Anthony, the protector of marriages; was thought to be the symbol of the Virgin Mary; and was a sacred symbol of Venus, the Roman goddess of love and beauty. Roman mythology also associates it with Juno, the queen of the gods and goddess of marriage. According to the myth, when Juno was nursing her son Hercules, excess milk fell from the sky. Part of it stayed in the heavens, creating the Milky Way, and part of it fell to earth, creating the lilies. In Rome, lilies were known as *Rosa junonis*, or Juno's rose. White lilies have always been considered a symbol of peace.

Romans used a concoction made from the bulbs to treat corns and sores on their feet, and they probably carried the plants to England with them for this purpose. Lily and yarrow, together boiled in oil, were used for burns, and lily seeds taken in drink were supposed to cure a snakebite. White lilies were thought to cure the bite of a mad dog. The bulbs, beaten with honey and placed on the face, were thought to clear the complexion and make facial wrinkles disappear. Washing hair often with lilies, ashes, and lye supposedly would turn the hair a blond color.

Though their medicinal properties were valuable and varied, lilies were soon appreciated for their beauty as well as their curative powers.

The Madonna lily was particularly popular in the sixteenth-century garden, though it did not receive this name until the end of the nineteenth century. It was a symbol of purity and innocence, and during the Middle Ages artists frequently painted female saints holding the blossoms.

Lilies have always been popular as decorations in the church. During Victorian times, however, some of the Christian churches removed the stamens and pistils so as not to offend anyone.

According to Anglo-Saxon folklore, if you offered an expectant mother both a rose and a lily, and she chose a rose, the baby would be a girl; if the lily was chosen, a boy was on the way. The lily is considered the sacred flower of motherhood. European superstition held that lilies were protection against witchcraft and kept ghosts from entering the garden.

Before the French Revolution, the House of Orange in Holland used the orange lily as a political symbol. When the House of Orange fell, in an act of defiance, radicals destroyed all lily bulbs.

Lilies are edible and even tasty. One suggestion for lily cuisine is to add fresh lily buds to clear chicken soup during the last three minutes of cooking for a bit of "lily-drop" soup.

The Sego lily is the state flower of Utah.

COMMON NAME: **lily of the valley**
GENUS: *Convallaria*
SPECIES, HYBRIDS, CULTIVARS: *C. mahalis fortunei* 'Giant Bells'—up to fifteen large bells; grows 8 to 10 inches tall; suitable for forcing; will bloom approximately three weeks after being planted.
FAMILY: Liliaceae
BLOOMS: spring
TYPE: perennial
DESCRIPTION: Flower stalks are arching and hold ten to fifteen fragrant, white, bell-shaped blossoms. The stems are strong, which helps to make this a good cut flower. Large ribbed leaves clasp the stem.
CULTIVATION: Top-coat plants with a dressing of manure each fall, and fertilize heavily. Lily of the valley should be planted in well-drained soil that is rich in organic matter. Plant the small pips horizontally, 2 inches deep, 3 inches apart, and be sure to place them in an area that gets plenty of moisture. Light shade or well-filtered sun give this plant the best lighting conditions. Lily of the valley spreads from year to year and is easy to grow.

Native to most European countries, lily of the valley is a favorite of people everywhere. It is cherished and revered in many countries for its symbolism and folklore.

A medieval Christian legend of the origin of lily of the valley told of Saint Leonard, a close friend of King Clovis of France (of the iris legend). Though a brave and fearless fighter, Saint Leonard was something of a recluse and found life at court unappealing. In A.D. 559 he asked permission to go live in the woods so he could spend his days among the trees and flowers communing with God. The dragon Temptation, who also lived in those woods, was furious that Saint Leonard had invaded his privacy. He appeared to Saint Leonard one day, in the form of a dragon, demanding that he leave the woods. Leonard was at prayer and did not hear him, so this devil dragon went to Saint Leonard's hut and burned it down with his fiery breath. When Saint Leonard returned, he fought the dragon. It was a fierce battle, and much blood was spilled. Wherever the dragon lost a drop of blood, a poisonous weed began to grow. Wherever Saint Leonard's blood fell, a lily of the valley appeared. After three days, Saint Leonard was finally able to slay the dragon.

Much symbolism involves lily of the valley. It is considered the sign of Christ's second coming, and is often called ladder to heaven or Jacob's tears. The plant is also mentioned in the Song of Solomon in the Bible. Mary's tears is yet another name for lily of the valley; legend says that when Mary cried at the cross, her tears turned into this flower. It is considered a symbol of purity and humility, sweetness, and renewed happiness. In some areas, lily of the valley was thought to have the power to help men envision a better world.

Lily of the valley was used extensively for medicine. Several elaborate recipes exist for creating concoctions from the plant. One of these was written by John Gerard, a sixteenth-century English botanist. He said that if you put blossoms from lily of the valley into a glass, set the glass in an anthill, and cover it up for one month, the liquid found in the glass after this time would be invaluable for treating the "paine and griefe of the gout." A similar recipe is in the first chapter of Robert Louis Stevenson's *Kidnapped*. A recipe that is a bit easier to carry out calls for soaking one-half pound of the flowers in a liter of wine for four weeks. This creates a liquor that was considered more precious than gold. Smeared on the forehead and the back of the neck, it was thought to make one have good common sense.

Another early botanist suggested that the flowers, distilled in wine, would restore speech "unto those that have the dum palsie." The flowers, dipped in wine and eaten, were thought to relieve migraine headaches. Lily of the valley was also used to treat eye inflammations, to strengthen memory, and as a love potion. The medicinal power of the plant was thought to be so strong that infusions made from it were kept in gold and silver vessels.

Despite its reputed powers, all parts of the plant are considered somewhat poisonous. It, like the foxglove, contains substances that are used to strengthen the heart. It should never be used without first consulting a doctor. It is sometimes used to treat patients recovering from a stroke, and it seems to be particularly effective at helping to restore speech.

Occasionally called glovewort, lily of the valley was used to treat sore or chapped hands.

The genus name is from the Latin word for valley and perhaps refers to the original home of the plant, though it can be found growing naturally in many different habitats.

Lily of the valley, cultivated for over 400 years, seems to be loved everywhere. Sprigs of the blossoms are worn in the lapel on May Day in France, and it is the national flower of Finland. In Germany and Scandinavian countries, it was thought to be good luck to go to the woods and pick "Virgin's tears" in the spring.

Often carried in bridal bouquets, lily of the valley is sometimes considered the "fifth thing" that a bride should carry (right after something old, something new, something borrowed, something blue). The Dutch carry this a bit further and often plant the pips of lily of the valley in the first garden the couple owns. Each time the plants bloom, year after year, the couple is supposed to celebrate the renewal of their love.

Lily of the valley leaves make a good dye, changing cloth to either yellow or green, depending on what season of the year the leaves are gathered.

COMMON NAME: **narcissus**
GENUS: *Narcissus*
SPECIES, HYBRIDS, CULTIVARS:
daffodils—'King Alfred,' all yellow; 'Mount
Hood,' white; 'Pink Glory,' white and pink.
Jonquils—'Treuithian,' pale yellow; 'Suzy,'
yellow and orange red. Other
narcissi—'Duke of Windsor,' white petals and
orange apricot cup; 'Ice Follies,' heavy
bloomer that is white with lemon yellow
cup.
FAMILY: Amaryllidaceae
TYPE: Perennial
BLOOMS: spring
DESCRIPTION: A daffodil is a narcissus
with a trumpet that is as long or longer than
the surrounding petals. The trumpet is
usually flared and is often a different color or
shade from the petals. Only one flower is
found on a single stem. Other narcissi have
shallow center cups or trumpets. Colors
range through all the yellow tones and into
pinks and oranges. Jonquils (*N. jonquilla*)
have clusters of flowers, each with a shallow
cup whose color contrasts with the petals.
CULTIVATION: Narcissi are hardy and
easy to grow. They like full or half-day sun
but do almost as well in shady areas.
Although they prefer rich, moist soil, they
cannot tolerate standing water. Allow the
foliage to die back naturally. Cut it too soon,
and you will rob the bulb of essential food
sources, and it might die. After the plants
have flowered, top-dress the bulbs with a
5-10-5 fertilizer. Choose early, mid-season,
and late-blooming varieties to extend the
blooming season.

Greek mythology tells us how narcissus
plants came to be: Echo was a mountain
nymph who fell madly in love with a
beautiful young man, Narcissus. Narcissus
was a vain youth and cared for nothing but
his own beauty. He spent all his time looking
at his own reflection in a pool of water and
spurned Echo's love until she finally faded
away, leaving nothing but her voice. The
gods, angry with Narcissus because of his
vanity, changed him into a flower who was
destined always to sit by a pool nodding at
his own reflection.

Similar versions of this myth occur in
Rome, Arabia, Egypt, Spain, and Portugal.

Another Greek myth tells of Proserpina,
who was kidnapped by the god Pluto while
she was gathering lilies. As Pluto carried her
to the underworld, she dropped the liles;
when they fell to the earth, they became
daffodils, hanging their heads for her sorrow.

Mythology also suggests that Venus
governs all daffodils except the yellow, and
that belongs to Mars.

In the Orient, narcissus is known as the
sacred lily of China. It is the symbol of
purity and promise and is the floral emblem
of the Chinese New Year.

The name daffodil has a hazy origin. It
could, perhaps, come from the fact that
Norman soldiers thought daffodils were
similar to asphodel flowers (members of the
Lily family), and the name has changed from
d'asphodel to daffodil. Another possible
origin of the word is from an old English
word, affodyle, which means "that which
comes early."

Jonquil (the name of a favorite species)
has a more precise beginning, for the native
narcissus in Spain was called *juncas*, from
the Latin word for rush, since the leaves
looked similar to rushes. The Spanish called
it *junquillo* and the French, *jonquille*. The
jump from that to the English jonquil was
easy.

*N. jonquilla* has been called Queen
Anne's jonquil because of this English queen's
love for this particular flower. She did
excellent needlework and wove patterns of
jonquil blossoms into tapestries, carpets, and
dresses. It was her love of jonquils that

inspired Queen Anne to establish Kensington Palace Gardens, the first public gardens in England.

Wild daffodils caused the first wildlife protective legislation in England. The flowers were so popular in the Stuart court that peasants and gypsies would go to the fields and pick them by the thousand to sell at court. This depletion of the native plant population caused a public protest, and laws were passed to protect the flowers.

Traditionally the first Sunday in April in England was "Daffodil Sunday," and people would pick daffodils from their homes and surrounding fields to take to the hospitals in London.

Though narcissus bulbs are poisonous, they have been used medicinally for centuries. A doctor named Galen was surgeon at the school of gladiators in Rome. His favorite salve to "glue together great wounds, cuts, and gashes" was the juice from narcissus bulbs. The bulbs are said to have been a standard bit of medication in the first-aid bags of Roman soldiers. European peasants would mix the juice with honey and apply it to cuts or swollen joints.

The word narcissus is from the Greek word *narkeo*, meaning "to be stupified," and this alludes to the poisonous properties of the plant. The bulbs contain lycorcine which paralyzes the heart and numbs the nervous system.

Scientists are testing chemicals from narcissus bulbs as a possible treatment for multiple sclerosis.

Though no narcissus is native to North America, this has not hampered its popularity here. Every year millions of bulbs are bought and planted, and the blooms are sniffed and cherished by Americans all across the country.

Superstition in Maine says that if you point at a daffodil with your index finger, you will cause it not to bloom.

In the Victorian language of flowers, a daffodil means regard, and the great yellow daffodil is the symbol of chivalry. Narcissus is the Chinese symbol of good fortune and the emblem of winter. In Japan, it is the symbol of mirth and joyousness and the emblem of formality.

The love of narcissus is ancient. Mohammed is said to have said, "Let him who hath two loaves sell one, and buy the flower of narcissus: for bread is but food for the body, whereas narcissus is food for the soul."

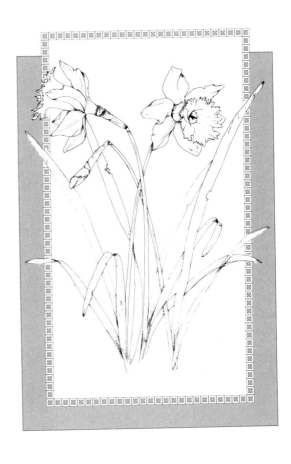

COMMON NAME: peony
GENUS: *Paeonia*
SPECIES, HYBRIDS, CULTIVARS:
*P. lactiflora* (Chinese peony)—many
hybrids; single or double. *P. suffruticosa*
(tree peony)—shrub; does not die back in
winter.
FAMILY: Ranunculaceae
BLOOMS: late spring
TYPE: perennial
DESCRIPTION: Peony greets spring
with offerings of very large, beautiful
blossoms in pinks, white, and shades of red.
The foliage is neat and attractive, and the
plants create an appealing, low (2½ to 3
foot) shrub during the summer months.
Peony flowers are full and measure 4 to 6
inches across.
CULTIVATION: Probably one of the
greatest attributes of peonies is their
longevity. Some peony plants are reported to
be more than 100 years old. Once
established, peonies should not be
transplanted. The plants are tolerant of a
wide range of soils but will perform best in
neutral or slightly alkaline soils that are light,
fertile, and rich in organic matter. Peony
roots should be planted so that the eyes are
exactly 1½ inches below the soil level. Mix
in generous amounts of humus or peat moss
before planting. In northern areas, plant in
full sun. In hot southern climates, provide a
bit of shade.

Called the blessed herb, peonies have been
used for centuries for their magical and
medicinal properties. Among the powers that
peony was thought to possess are the ability
to protect shepherds and their flocks; to
ward off storms, demons, and nightmares;
and to preserve the harvest from danger.
Peony is the Greek symbol of healing and the
Japanese symbol for a happy marriage and
virility. It is the Japanese floral emblem for
the month of June.

The Chinese have grown this flower for
over 2,000 years. The name for it there is
*Sho-yo*, which means "the beautiful," and it
is considered the flower of prosperity. One
Chinese emperor called peonies roses of
spring, and a single specimen sold for as
much as 100 ounces of gold. According to
the Chinese calendar, the tree peony is the
floral symbol for March.

The medicinal powers of the plant are
legendary. It was named for Paeon, physician
to the Greek gods, and a student of Asclepius
(god of medicine and healing). Leto, goddess
of fertility, told Paeon about a magical root
growing on Mount Olympus that would
soothe the pain of women in childbirth.
When Paeon went to get this root, Asclepius
became jealous and angry and threatened to
kill his pupil. Leto begged help from Zeus,
who saved Paeon from the wrath of his
teacher by changing him into the peony
flower.

Perhaps because of this legend, peony
seeds have been given to pregnant women
for centuries. It was also thought that the
roots, held over a person's head or around
the neck, would cure insanity. Other
medicinal uses included the prevention of
epileptic convulsions and soothing the gums
of teething infants. Pliny, a Roman statesman,
said that peonies are the "oldest of plants,
and are an important medicine that cures
twenty ills."

Superstition warns us, however, that the
plant is protected by woodpeckers. If you try
to gather peony for medicinal purposes
while a woodpecker is in sight, your patient
might die.

The magical powers of peonies were
thought to be even stronger than the
medicinal ones. Mothers in rural areas hung
strings of peony seeds around an infant's
neck as protection against the "Evil Eye."

The seeds, particularly if soaked in rain water, were worn as an amulet for protection against witchcraft and the devil. The plant's reputation for supernatural powers was enhanced by its phosphorescent qualities—some plants actually glow in the dark. For the most potent magical powers, seeds and roots were gathered in the dead of night.

The first peonies, considered important healing herbs, were brought to England by the Roman legions in 1200. They have been cherished in England since then, first for their medicinal value, and then for their unparalleled beauty. Peonies have been in the United States since early colonial days. For the Philadelphia Centennial Exposition in 1876, peony was used to symbolize the American spirit, ambition, and determination to adapt and thrive.

The only country ever named for a flower was Paeonia, located in what is now northern Greece. It was a legitimate country complete with government, army, and imperial ring, but it was conquered during the Persian Wars.

Peony is the state flower of Indiana.

The language of peony is shame, for it was thought to be the hiding place of a dishonorable nymph.

COMMON NAME:  **poppy**
GENUS:  *Papaver*
SPECIES:  *P. nudicaule*—Iceland poppy.
*P. rhoeas*—Shirley or corn poppy; blooms
spring and summer. *P. orientale*—huge,
bowl-shaped blossoms; perennial.
FAMILY:  *Papaveraceae*
BLOOMS:  late spring, summer
TYPE:  annual, perennial
DESCRIPTION:  Iceland poppy is a
tender perennial, usually grown as an annual.
The leaves are finely dissected, fernlike, and
hairy. The large blossoms (3 inches across)
come in orange, red, pink, rose, yellow,
cream, and white. Oriental poppy has huge
blossoms—sometimes as much as 12 inches
across—with a black center. Plants grow 2 to
4 feet tall. Corn or Shirley poppy is usually
grown as an annual and reaches a height of 2
to 5 feet. Colors include red, orange, and
pink in both single and double forms.
CULTIVATION:  Disliking hot, humid
weather, poppies do best in cool climates in
alkaline soil that is well drained but not too
rich. Water them moderately and place them
in full sun. Keep blossoms picked to
stimulate further flowering. Set out plants in
early spring or sow seeds in late spring for
bloom in late summer or early fall.

Poppies have been grown for beauty, magic,
and medicine for centuries. Egyptians felt
that poppies were a necessary part of
funerals and burial rituals and were essential
for assuring life after death. Dried poppy
petals have been found in tombs dating back
3,000 years.

Early Romans used juice from the poppy
plant for witchcraft. It was thought to be
particularly effective in easing the pains of
love.

Ancient Greeks thought that poppies
were a sign of fertility and placed garlands of
poppy blossoms at the shrines of Demeter,
goddess of fertility, and Diana, goddess of
the hunt. The Greeks also used poppy seeds
as a love charm and for seasoning in breads
and drinks. Poppy seeds were thought to
bring strength and health, and Greek
Olympic athletes were given mixtures of
poppy seeds, honey, and wine.

During the Middle Ages, tea made from
the dried petals was used to calm children
suffering from colic or whooping cough.
Poppy syrup was used in Elizabethan
England to relieve pain and induce sleep. Tea
made from the poppy plant was thought to
be good for rheumatism, particularly if it
was mixed with white wine.

Country girls in Europe played
fortune-telling games with petals from
poppies. Placing a poppy petal in her lover's
hand, a girl would hit it with the edge of her
own hand. If a loud popping noise resulted,
it meant he was true to her. If the petal broke
silently, it meant that he had been unfaithful.

Poppy is the English flower for August
and the Chinese floral emblem for the month
of December. It is the symbol of consolation
and denotes sleep, rest, and repose.

The corn poppy, *P. rhoeas*, is native to
the Mediterranean areas of Europe, does not
contain opium, and is not a source of
narcotic drugs, as are the Oriental poppies.
The plant does contain a substance,
rhoeadine, that is nonpoisonous and has
been used as a mild sedative. A concoction
made from this plant was used to prevent
wrinkled skin. The petals can be placed in
boiling water and steeped for about ten
minutes, strained, and stored to be used as a
skin freshener.

Today the greatest culinary demand for
poppies is for their seeds, which are tasty
baked in breads and cakes.

The flowers provide a rather unstable
dye but one that is suitable for coloring

wines and other drinks, as well as inks and medicines.

The corn poppy is most famous as an emblem that commemorates those who died in wars. This custom began after World War I when thousands of poppies bloomed on the battlefields of Flanders. Not to detract from the magic of this occurrence, but poppies had grown in Flanders fields for many centuries. During the war, the earth had been so trampled down that nothing was able to grow. Seeds of the poppies lay dormant but viable during this time, and when peace returned to the land and the grass and flowers were allowed to grow once more, the poppies burst forth in great profusion. Actual soil counts were done, and it was found that as many as 2,500 poppy seeds could be found in a single square foot. The magical wave of corn poppies was immortalized by the poem by John McCrae, "In Flanders Fields."

In 1921 England celebrated Poppy Day. On this day, thousands of artificial poppies were made and sold to families of war veterans.

The origin of the genus name, *Papaver*, could be from the word pap, which is ground food given to infants. Pap often included juice from the poppy plant to help the babies sleep. Another possibility is that papaver is the word the Celts used to describe the sound made by the Roman soldiers eating poppy seeds. The species name *rhoeas* means "to fall," for the petals of this plant fall off quite easily.

Shirley poppy is a hybrid developed by a vicar from Shirley, England. Reverend William Wilkes was not only an accomplished plant breeder, but also an enthusiastic rural naturalist.

If treated correctly, poppies make a good cut flower. Full buds that have straight stems should be cut in the evening and submerged up to their necks in hot water.

The popular little California poppy is of the same family but a different genus. Its bright orange and yellow faces light up the fields and roadsides along the West Coast and can be found growing in gardens in nearly every part of the country.

COMMON NAME: **primrose**
GENUS: *Primula*
SPECIES, HYBRIDS, CULTIVARS:
*P. denticulata*—lavender, purple, or white flowers; grows to 12 inches. *P. japonica* 'Millar Crimson'—flowers whorled around 24-inch stem; blooms May-June.
*P. polyanthus*—best known; colors are red, pink, blue, gold, and white, all with small yellow eyes.
FAMILY: Primulaceae
BLOOMS: spring
TYPE: perennial
DESCRIPTION: Primroses form an attractive rosette of crinkly, light green leaves. The flowers are generally brightly colored and occur in tight bundles on individual stems above the leaves.
CULTIVATION: Needing partial shade, primroses thrive in well-drained, rich soil. They are indigenous to cool, moist meadows and woodland environments. Duplicating these conditions as closely as possible will create the best growing conditions for primroses. The soil should not be allowed to dry completely. To retain vigorously blooming plants, divide clumps every four to five years. Seeds should be sown in midsummer for bloom the following spring.

Primrose is beloved by people everywhere, but is particularly cherished by the English. Buckner Hollingsworth, in his book *Flower Chronicles*, proclaims that "England displays a rose on the royal coat of arms, but she carries a primrose in her heart."

Primrose is a symbol of early youth, and to walk down the primrose path meant a life of pleasure and self-indulgence. According to English folk legends, the primrose was a symbol for wantonness. The word primrose was also thought to mean "most excellent."

The name primrose is from the Latin word *primus*, meaning "first," and was given to this plant because it is among the first flowers to bloom in spring.

Common names for the plant abound. In Germany it is known as *Himmelschusslechen*, meaning "little keys to heaven." Other names similar to this include our Lady's key, marriage key, the key flower, Virgins' keys, and Saint Peter's keys. It was thought that primrose had the magical power to open treasure chests, or even better, to open rocks to reveal hidden treasure. The references to keys stem from the resemblance of the cluster of flowers to a bunch of keys. According to a German legend, Saint Peter heard a rumor that some wayward souls were trying to slip into the backdoor of heaven rather than enter through the Pearly Gates. He got so upset he dropped the keys to heaven, and where they landed on earth, they grew into primroses.

Other names for primrose refer to a mystical connection with fairies and elves and include such appellations as fairy flower, fairy cup, or fairy basins. Fairies were thought to take shelter under primrose leaves during a rainstorm.

Cowslip is a favorite English name for the primrose. Although there is some question as to how the plant came to be known by this name, most people agree that cowslip probably came from cow slop. Since the plants grew so abundantly in fields, the superstition arose that they must have sprung from cow dung.

Primroses have been used since medieval times to cure a wide variety of ailments. Called *herba paralysis*, it was considered good for those suffering from gout. According to a fourteenth century herbal, to "put the juice of 'primerose' into a man's mouth would restore lost speech." Mountain climbers in Switzerland carried the primrose root for its supposed powers to combat vertigo. The plant has also been used to cure convulsions, hysteria, neck and muscular pains, and coughs. Water distilled from an infusion of leaves and flowers was said to be good for "pain in the head from a cold, the biting of mad dogs, and women that beareth a child." Eating primrose leaves in a salad was thought to be good for arthritis. A book on household remedies published in 1898 suggested that an ointment made from primrose leaves would be good on burns and ulcers.

In addition to its use as a medicine, primrose has also enjoyed quite a reputation as a beauty aid. Culpeper, a seventeenth-century English physician, wrote that "our city dames know well enough the ointment or distilled water of it (primrose) adds to beauty, or at least restores it when it is lost." Ointment from the common English cowslip, *P. veris*, was used to remove spots and wrinkles from the face. Primrose was used as rouge. It was thought that the leaf, if rubbed on the cheek of a fair-skinned woman, would cause a red glow.

Primroses can also be used in the kitchen. The leaves and flowers are eaten raw in salads, or they can be mixed with other herbs and used to stuff poultry. The leaves and flowers add flavor and color to many foods, particularly egg or custard dishes. Tea can be made from the dried or fresh petals. Steep the petals in boiling water for several minutes, strain, and enjoy. Juice from the flowers can also be made into tasty country wine, jams, jellies, and preserves. Pickles and conserves were also made from the blossoms.

In the 1880s, April 19 in England was declared Primrose Day. This was in honor of Benjamin Disraeli (English prime minister from 1874 to 1880), for the primrose was his favorite flower and this was his birthday.

Primrose is considered the flower of February.

COMMON NAME: snapdragon
GENUS: *Antirrhinum*
SPECIES: *A. majus*
FAMILY: Scrophulariaceae
BLOOMS: late spring
TYPE: annual
DESCRIPTION: Snapdragons have delighted many generations of children with their brightly colored mouths that open when the flowers are pressed on the sides. Flowers are borne on long stalks and occur in all colors except blue. The flowers open at the bottom of the stalk first. Plant breeders have enjoyed working with this flower, and it is now possible to get snapdragons in a variety of heights (from 8 to 36 inches), colors, and flower forms.
CULTIVATION: Snapdragons will do best in well-drained soils located in full sun. They like abundant amounts of calcium, neutral soils, regular watering, and periodic feedings with a liquid fertilizer. Plant seeds indoors in late winter, or sow seeds directly into the flower beds in spring.

———— ❧ ————

Many common names for this plant refer to the shape of the blossom. Toad's mouth, dog's mouth, or lion's mouth all refer to the fact that if you squeeze the blossom in just the right way, the petals open to reveal a yawning mouth. The seed pods look a bit like a nose or a snout, and this has given rise to names like calves' snout. The botanical name also refers to this characteristic, for *Antirrhinum* is from two Greek words, *anti*, meaning "like," and *rhinos*, meaning "snout."

Snapdragon is native to southern Europe and is now naturalized in many places in Europe. In Mediterranean areas the plants were once cultivated for the seeds, which contain high amounts of oil. Though of poorer quality, this oil was used like olive oil. Superstition said that he who was anointed with the oil of snapdragon would become famous.

The plant has no medicinal value, but the oil from the seeds was supposed to ward off witchcraft and sorcery.

Snapdragon depends almost entirely on bumblebees for pollination. Because of the design of the blossom, honey bees are not heavy enough to pollinate it successfully.

The brightly colored blossoms are good for dyeing cloth.

COMMON NAME:  stock
GENUS:  *Matthiola*
SPECIES, HYBRIDS, CULTIVARS:
*M. incana* 'Trysomic Seven
Weeks'—blooms in seven weeks from seed.
FAMILY:  Cruciferae
BLOOMS:  spring
TYPE:  annual
DESCRIPTION:  Stock is as easy to
identify from its perfume as from its
appearance. The fragrance is strong and
spicy. Flowering stalks are 2 to 3 feet tall and
bear many large blossoms. Colors include
white, yellow, pink, rose, purple, and
lavender.
CULTIVATION:  Sow stock seeds
outdoors in a sunny spot with light,
well-drained soil that is high in fertility. In
areas with a mild climate, seeds can be sown
in late fall. Water the plants regularly.

———— ❧ ————

Wild stock has grown on the southern coast
of the Isle of Wight for centuries. Sea-going
men used the leaves and roots on their
voyages to ward off scurvy, for stock is high
in vitamins.

The botanical name reflects the
medicinal value of stock, for the genus was
named for an Italian botanist and physician,
Pietro Andrea Matthioli (1501–1577), who
wrote many papers and books on medicinal
botany. He was royal physician to Roman
Emperor Maximilian II and used stock only
for "matters of love and lust." The common
name comes from the Latin word *stoce*,
which means "trunk or stick," and is,
perhaps, descriptive of the straight flowering
stalk.

This plant was often found growing
within ancient castle walls. Manuscripts
dating back to 1578 describe stock; one
praises the "beautie of the flowers and
pleasant sweete smell." The fragrance of the
flowers is still quite pleasing, particularly that
of the night scented stock, *M.bicornis*. Its
scent fills the air, making the garden a place
of magic in the early evening.

In the late 1600s, gardeners believed
they would get the fullest blooms from this
plant by sowing the seeds in April on a night
when the moon was full. On the next full
moon, they dug up the seedlings, added sand
to the earth, and replanted them
immediately.

During Elizabethan times, stock was
known as stock-gilloflowers. Gilloflowers
was a favorite name for carnation, and the
scent of stock is similar to that of carnations.
Shakespeare wrote of "streaked gillovors,"
obviously referring to cultivated bicolored
forms.

Purple stock makes a wonderful blue
dye, and all colors make good cut flowers.

COMMON NAME: **tulip**
GENUS: *Tulipa*
SPECIES, HYBRIDS, CULTIVARS:
The most commonly used hybrid tulips are
Darwin, Darwin hybrid, cottage, breeder,
multi-flowered, and lily flowered. Popular
species tulips include *T. kaufmanniana,*
*T. fosteriana, T. praestaus, T. greigii,*
*T. kolpakowskiana,* and *T. pulchella.*
FAMILY: Liliaceae
BLOOMS: late spring
TYPE: perennial
DESCRIPTION: Though there is
tremendous variation in color and color
patterns, the basic flower form of the tulip,
that of six petals and broad green leaves,
remains the same.
CULTIVATION: Full sun or partial
shade and rich, well-aerated soil, amended
with organic matter or leaf mold, provide
good growing conditions for tulips. The
bulbs should be planted 2 to 4 inches deep
in autumn. They like very cold weather. In
mild climates, flowering will not be good
year after year, and tulips are often treated as
an annual bulb.

Tulips are probably one of the first flowers
cultivated solely for their beauty. Tulip
designs are found on pottery jars dated from
2200 to 1600 B.C., and tulips were found on
the border of a ninth-century Byzantine
fabric. Though they must have been known
to them, tulips were not mentioned at all by
Greek or Roman writers.

European explorers and traders found
tulips growing in the gardens of Turkish
sultans in the early 1500s. They were of such
beauty that in 1554 the Austrian ambassador,
Ghislain de Busbecq, acquired some of the
bulbs at a great price and took them back to
Vienna. He gave them to Flemish botanist
Charles de Lecluse and inadvertently planted
the seed of tulipmania in Holland.

After a period of about twenty years, de
Lecluse took a teaching post in the
Netherlands and took some of the seeds and
bulbs of tulips there. Although he had
intended to sell them to plump up his slim
pocketbook, the tulip bulbs were stolen, and
soon tulips were growing throughout the
country.

By 1634 tulipmania had hit Holland.
Enthusiasm over the bulbs reached fever
pitch, and their price per pound was often
more than that of precious metal. When
interest in the solid-colored flowers began to
wane somewhat, breeders began producing
unusual blossoms, because striped, feathered,
and marbled varieties brought higher prices.
Stripes and some other coloration are
actually caused by a virus and not a
mutation, making it impossible to get the
same coloration from seed. These must be
bred from an offshoot of the parent bulb.

One bulb of the variety 'Semper
Augustus' is said to have sold for a record
price of 5,500 florins, today's equivalent of
about $2,500.

Many Dutch citizens were extremely
wealthy during this time and had large and
lavish gardens at their summer estates. Tulips
became a status symbol, as each family tried
to outdo the next in the number and variety
of tulips growing in their gardens.

In 1637 traders and dealers began to
realize that bulb prices were artificially high
and did not reflect the actual value of the
bulbs. As the tulip market toppled, the result
was economic depression and true hunger
and poverty in many areas. Especially hard
hit were the many farmers who, hoping for a
quick fortune, had begun to grow tulips
instead of food.

Learning from the mistakes made by the
Dutch, the Turkish government passed strict
laws during the "Age of Tulips" in Turkey
between 1703 and 1730. Bulbs could be
bought and sold only in the capital city, and
punishment for breaking this law was exile.

The government also kept careful records, and at one time these records indicated that the Turks had over 1,550 varieties of tulips.

One story is told of an English trader who received a shipment of cloth from Turkey. Along with the cloth was what he thought were onions. He ate some of them and enjoyed them so much he asked his gardener to plant them in the vegetable garden. Imagine his surprise when he found the glorious tulip blossoms growing among the vegetables the next spring.

Tulip bulbs are quite edible and some even call them tasty. They can be substituted in any recipe for onions. One recipe for tulip-tomato sauce calls for sautéing two minced tulip bulbs with parsley and garlic, then adding four cups of chopped tomatoes and simmering for one hour. The stamens and ovaries, sautéed in butter, are supposedly quite good, tasting something like asparagus.

Tulips were first brought to America by the Dutch colonists who settled in the northeastern part of the country. The popularity of these flowers in those communities is obvious from the prevalence of the tulip in Pennsylvania Dutch designs from the period.

The name tulip is derived from the name for the Turkish hat, turban. When traders and visitors came to Turkey to see the famous gardens, the gardeners kept pointing out that tulip blossoms resembled upside-down turbans, or tulibands, as the Turkish called them. Soon visitors began to refer to these flowers as tulibands, and this was eventually changed to tulip.

A Persian legend tells of the origin of tulips. A young man, Farhad, was in love with a beautiful woman, Sharin. One day Farhad received news that his lover was dead. In his grief, he jumped off a high cliff, and where his body landed, there the tulips first began to grow. The saddest part was that the message was sent by a jealous rival, and Sharin was actually still alive.

Tulips are indigenous to the northern temperate zones from the Mediterranean coast east to Japan. *T. sharonensis*, or the Sharon tulip, is thought to be the "rose of Sharon" mentioned in the Song of Solomon in the Bible. The Sharon tulip grows on the Plain of Sharon, found between Carmel and Jaffa.

Tulips are considered the symbol of perfect love, and the Turks used them as a love potion. If a tulip was given to a girl, the color of the petals determined the meaning of the flower. Red petals meant a declaration of love. Yellow petals meant hopeless love, and variegated petals meant beautiful eyes. A black center meant a heart burned from love.

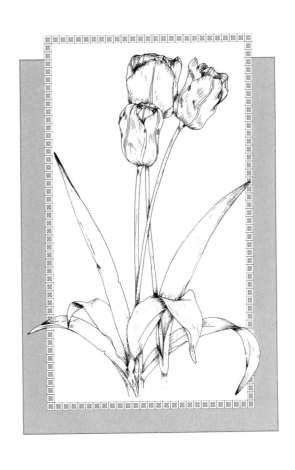

COMMON NAME: vinca
GENUS: *Vinca*
SPECIES: *V. major, V. minor;*
both perennial
FAMILY: Apocynaceae
BLOOMS: spring
TYPE: perennial
DESCRIPTION: Perennial vinca is a fast-spreading vine with blue flowers. *V. major* is a more vigorous grower and has larger leaves and flowers. The annual bedding plant vinca (actually *Catharanthus roseus*) has attractive five-petaled white and pink-to-red flowers and dark green, glossy leaves. The plants reach a height of 10 to 15 inches and spread almost 2 feet across.
CULTIVATION: Annual vinca (*C. roseus)* is extremely heat and drought tolerant and thrives in full, hot sun. It blooms prolifically from early summer until frost. Perennial vinca is particularly useful as a ground cover, because it grows equally as well in sun or shade. Blooming, which occurs in late spring, is much better in the sun, however.

Twelve species of this genus are native to Europe. *V. major*, also known as greater periwinkle, blue buttons, and band plant, and *V. minor*, known as common periwinkle, lesser periwinkle, and running myrtle, are the two species most widely grown.

Rosy periwinkle, a tropical species, contains an alkaloid necessary to make the drug vincristine, which is used to treat many forms of cancer.

The popular pink and white vinca used as a bedding plant is officially *C. roseus*, though it was known for many years as *V. rosea*. It is native from Madagascar to India and is known as rose periwinkle and old maid.

Vinca has been cultivated for centuries. The number of common names alludes to the variety of purposes for which this plant has been used and particularly to the magical powers it was thought to possess. Known as devil's eye or sorcerer's violet, vinca blossoms were sometimes worn in the buttonhole as protection against witches. If placed over the doorway, vinca was thought to keep away witches.

During the Middle Ages criminals on the way to the gallows traditionally wore garlands made from vinca blossoms. The Italian name for the plant is flower of death, and it was often planted on the graves of children.

Belgians believed that the flower was a symbol of virginity and would spread vinca petals in front of bridal couples as they left the church.

It is from the pink and red vinca that the phrase "pink of perfection" originated. An old English book, *The Vertues of Herbes, Stones and Certain Beasts*, suggests that "Perwynke when it (the leaf) is beate unto powder with worms of ye earth wrapped about it and with an hearbe called houslyck it induceth love between man and wife if it be used in their meales."

Red vinca, also called joy of the ground, planted outside the garden gate symbolized an invitation to the passer-by to come in and look at the garden.

The medicinal uses of vinca are varied. Vinca tea made from the blossoms was used, according to an ancient herbal, if the "mother's milk was running too full." A tonic made from dried, full-grown leaves was used for intestinal problems. The leaves, mixed with other herbs, were thought to help diabetics. An ointment made from the leaves was used to treat skin disorders, particularly on the scalp, and the raw leaves were chewed to stop a nosebleed. The young shoots were boiled and eaten to prevent nightmares and to soothe nervous disorders and hysteria. Long strands of the creeping vine were wrapped tightly around the legs to ease muscular cramps. Perhaps the favorite reason for indulging in a daily dose of vinca was the superstition that it would help one be happy and comfortable and have grace.

Because it is evergreen, vinca has been chosen as the symbol of fidelity and friendship. The blue blossoms represent the pleasures of memory, red blossoms mean early friendship, and white blossoms are symbolic of pleasant recollections.

Vinca has been chosen by the city of Geneva as its floral emblem.

COMMON NAME: **wallflower**
GENUS: *Cheiranthus*
SPECIES: *C. allioni,, C. cheiri*
FAMILY: Cruciferae
BLOOMS: late spring–summer
TYPE: perennial
DESCRIPTION: Wallflowers come in lovely shades of orange, apricot, and yellow. Plants grow to a height of 14 to 18 inches. Numerous flowers occur at the ends of spikes. Leaves are long and narrow.
CULTIVATION: Wallflower plants cannot tolerate extreme heat and humidity. Given a sunny, airy spot in a mild climate, though, wallflower produce bright blossoms over a long period, if it is watered regularly. The plants grow easily from seed, which should be sown directly in the flowering site in spring. Blooms often come the first year from seed.

———— 🦋 ————

The following legend tells us of the origin of wallflower: The daughter of a Scottish lord fell in love with the son of an enemy border chieftain. The fathers, of course, took offense at the match, and the lord betrothed his daughter to a prince of his choosing and locked her up in a tower until the wedding was to take place. The chieftain's son, posing as a minstrel, sang at the foot of the tower, suggesting that she throw down a rope ladder and run away with him. The girl threw him a blossom of wallflower to indicate she understood and then began to climb down to her lover. Tragically, she slipped and fell to her death. The heartbroken young man adopted the wallflower as his emblem and wandered over the countryside singing of his beloved.

Because of this legend, wallflower is a symbol of faithfulness in adversity, according to the Victorian language of flowers. During the Middle Ages, troubadours and minstrels wore bunches of wallflower blossoms as a sign of good luck.

The genus name is from two Greek words meaning "hand" and "flower" and refers to the custom of carrying these sweet-scented flowers as a bouquet to ward off the evil odors resulting from poor sanitation practices of the past. They were especially popular during spring festivals.

The French call it *giroflee violier* because it has the same sweet scent as does the carnation, often called gilloflower.

The common name comes from the growth habit of some species, which prefer to climb stone walls or fences.

Wallflower has also been called blood drops of Christ, for the deep red wallflower was supposed to have grown under the cross. Also known as bloody warrior, wallflower was planted outside the cottage gate as protection against invaders.

Wallflower has always been valued as a medicine. Water of the distilled flowers, drunk twice a day for three to four weeks, was thought to make a woman fruitful. It has been used for uterine and liver disorders, to treat enlarged glands, and to purify the blood. Other remedies made from wallflowers have been used to ease pain during childbirth, treat palsy, and clear up cataracts. According to the doctorine of signatures, the yellow wallflower was used to treat jaundice. Scientists have discovered substances within the seeds, roots, and leaves that affect the heart, and for this reason it is not recommended for home remedy.

The plant was originally found growing in the Aegean islands.

# Summer

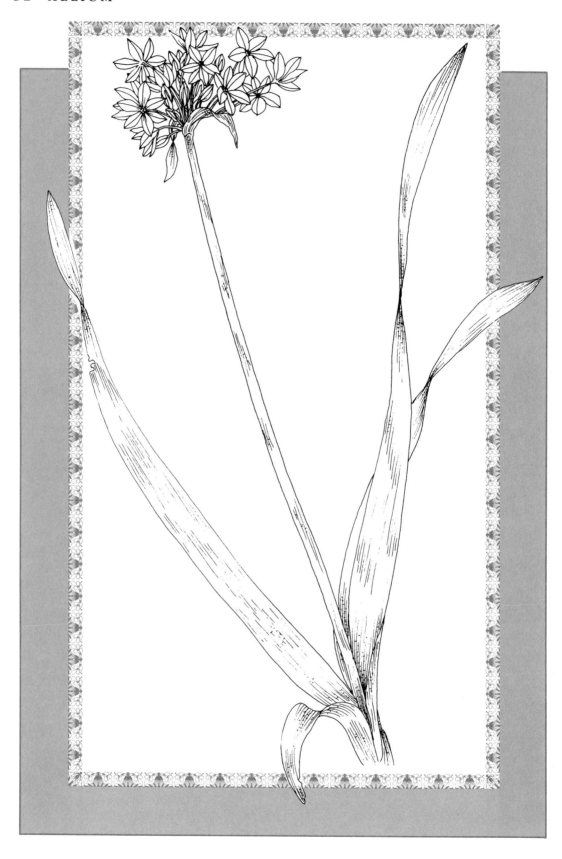

COMMON NAME: **allium**

GENUS: *Allium*

SPECIES, HYBRIDS, CULTIVARS:
*A. aflatunense*—stalks up to 24 to 30 inches; blooms in May. *A. albopilosum*—stems are 24 inches; lilac flower balls are 8 to 12 inches in diameter; blooms in June. *A. giganteum*—stems are 48 inches; flower balls are 5 inches across. *A. moly*—stems are 10 to 15 inches; flowers are in a loose cluster, yellow and star shaped. *A. neapolitanum grandiflorum*—white flowers on stems 10 inches tall. *A. ostrowskianum*—10 inches tall; red to pink flowers.

FAMILY: Amaryllidaceae

BLOOMS: summer

TYPE: perennial

DESCRIPTION: This genus shows a good bit of variation in flower size and plant height. *A. giganteum* flowers are huge, forming balls of lilac flowers that measure 5 inches across. The blossoms start off a light green, then turn a lovely lilac color, only to turn green again as they mature. They make a wonderful cut flower, lasting up to three weeks in water if clipped early. The plants get so tall they will probably need staking. This contrasts sharply with *A. moly*, which grows to a height of only 10 to 15 inches and has small yellow flowers.

CULTIVATION: Attractive and unusual, alliums grow from a bulb or bulblike rhizome. They like moderately rich, well-drained soil. Planting depth will vary according to the size of the bulb, which varies from one species to another. *A. aflatunense* should be planted 4 to 6 inches deep. *A. giganteum* bulbs should be planted 8 inches deep and 12 inches apart. *A. moly*, also known as golden garlic, should be planted close together, 4 inches deep. *A. ostrowskianum* is good for the rock garden and should be planted 5 inches deep, 12 inches apart.

The name allium comes from the Latin word for "onion," and if you were to bruise the leaves of any of these "flowering onions" you would immediately know why they earned this name. The fragrance of the blossoms of many species is quite pleasing, particularly that of the white allium, *A. neapolitanum*. The name allium could also have originated from the Celtic word *all*, meaning "pungent."

The small *A. moly* perhaps has the greatest amount of folklore associated with it. It is also called lily leek or golden garlic and, according to Homer, possesses magical qualities. It was this plant that kept Ulysses from being turned into a pig. According to the White Flower Farm catalog, many people still think this species brings "astounding good fortune and prosperity."

Pliny, a Roman statesman, considered allium an exceedingly precious plant because of its supposed powers as a charm and as protection against charms.

Elizabethan gardeners disdained alliums as garden plants, and their popularity has only recently begun to surge once again.

COMMON NAME:  **artemisia**
GENUS:  *Artemisia*
SPECIES, HYBRIDS, CULTIVARS:
*A. arbrotanum. A. ludoviciana albula*
'Silver King'—fragrant, silvery foliage to
about 36 inches.
FAMILY:  Compositae
BLOOMS:  foliage during summer
TYPE:  perennial
DESCRIPTION:  The soft gray green
foliage and neat mounding habit of artemisia
make it particularly welcomed in the
summer garden. The plant is not grown for
its flowers but for the foliage. The leaves are
small, finely dissected, and quite aromatic.
CULTIVATION:  Grow artemisia in full
sun and well-drained soil that is not too rich.
Excessive heat and moisture will take their
toll on artemisia. If this becomes a problem,
cut the plant back severely, and new growth
should then be good and healthy.

The heavy medicinal scent of artemisia
makes it easy to believe in the myriad of
magical and medicinal qualities attributed to
this plant. It is also known as southernwood,
lad's love, old man, wormwood, or
mugwort. This latter name is from the
Anglo-Saxon name for the plant, mucgwyrt.
Mucg is the name of a small gnatlike insect.
Artemisia, or mucgwyrt, was often used to
repel these pests. Pieces of the plant were
also put into the cupboard to keep away ants
or placed among woolen clothes to keep
away moths. Thomas Hyll, a
sixteenth-century English writer, suggested
that artemisia should be placed in the
garden, because "no adder will come into a
garden in which grow wormwood, mugwort,
and southernwood."

Artemisia has been used for medicine
for centuries by the Chinese, Europeans, and
American Indians. *A. absinthium*, a shrubby

member of this genus, has been used
medicinally for nearly 2,500 years.
Hippocrates said it helped lessen the
poisonous effects of alcohol. If drunk with
vinegar, artemisia "remedieth the strangling
that cometh of eating todestoles," according
to an ancient herbal. It supposedly had the
power to give protection from the evil eye,
the plague, lightning, and the bite of a sea
dragon. Mugwort tea was thought to relieve
all the pains of the body. North American
Indians used it to cure scurvy, jaundice, and
indigestion.

Saint John's belt is another name for the
plant, for it was believed that John the
Baptist carried this plant with him when he
was in the wilderness.

Artemisia is named for Artemis, Greek
goddess of the moon and the hunt. Bestowed
with her magical powers, the plant protected
mortals from pestilence and disease. It
supposedly held special magic for travelers
and could protect them from fatigue,
sunstroke, and wild beasts.

The greenish black oil taken from *A.
absinthium* was originally used to flavor
absinthe liqueur. This practice was outlawed
when it was discovered that the oil contains
toxins that cause delirium and hallucinations.

COMMON NAME: astilbe
GENUS: *Astilbe*
SPECIES, HYBRIDS, CULTIVARS:
*A. arendsii* 'Deutschland'—early; good for forcing; white; to 24 inches. *A.a.* 'Europa'—pink; to a height of 18 to 24 inches. *A.a.* 'Ostrich Plume'—salmon pink; to 24 to 36 inches. *A.a.* 'Finale'—light pink; blooms July and August; drought tolerant.
FAMILY: Saxifragaceae
BLOOMS: early summer
TYPE: perennial
DESCRIPTION: A graceful plant with arching or straight plumes of small flowers, astilbe comes in white and shades of reds and pinks. Foliage is dark green or bronze and finely cut. Depending on the variety, these plants grow from heights of 15 to 40 inches and spread approximately 15 inches across. They form neat clumps of compound fernlike leaves.
CULTIVATION: Partial shade or full sun with ample moisture and soil rich in compost or leaf mold are the conditions necessary to grow astilbes. To maintain healthy, freely blooming flowers, apply fertilizer every spring and give them plenty of water during dry periods. Cutting back the faded flowers will make the plant look more attractive and will extend the blooming period. Because the plants like abundant moisture, they will do well at the edge of a pond or lake. Plants should be divided every three years. This can be done in the fall or spring.

Astilbe adds wonderful color and texture to a shady garden. According to the *Standard Cyclopedia of Horticulture*, astilbes are very easy to force. Pot them in general potting soil, and provide generous amounts of water and temperatures ranging between 50 and 60 degrees Fahrenheit. When the sprays begin to show color, place the pots in a sunny window in a saucer and give frequent applications of liquid manure. They should bloom in ten to fourteen weeks.

———— ✾ ————

The name astilbe is from two Greek words *a*, meaning "without," and *stilbe*, meaning "lustre." This refers to the lack of sheen on the leaves of many species. Some species are also referred to as goat's beard.

COMMON NAME: **baby's breath**
GENUS: *Gypsophila*
SPECIES, HYBRIDS, CULTIVARS:
*G. paniculata*—single white blossoms; 36 inches. *G.p. 'Bristol Fairy'*—double white flowers; to 48 inches.
*G.p.* 'Perfecta'—largest flowers, double white; 36 to 48 inches. *G.p.* 'Pink Star'—double pink; 18 inches. *G.p.* 'Pink Fairy'—large, double pink; to 18 inches; blooms June-September.
FAMILY: Caryophyllaceae
BLOOMS: summer
TYPE: perennial and annual
DESCRIPTION: Perennial baby's breath is a multi-branched plant bearing a multitude of small, usually white, flowers. There are few leaves to interrupt the profusion of flowers, and stems are thin and wiry, adding to the airy effect of the plant. The many varieties available vary in height from 18 to 48 inches. Pink forms are also available. Double varieties are generally grafted, and the nodules, indicating the point of grafting, should be planted 1 inch below soil level. Double perennial baby's breath planted from seed will result in only 50 percent double flowers. To be sure of getting all double flowers, grafted species must be used.
CULTIVATION: Neutral or alkaline soil is essential for growing healthy baby's breath plants. If your soil is slightly acidic, ground limestone can be added to create more alkaline conditions. The soil must be well drained, and the plants will do best in full sun with ample moisture. Seeds can be sown from May 1 to July 15 outdoors in a flower bed or cold frame. Seedlings appearing during summer will need protection from the hot sun. Winter mulch is necessary in very cold climates.

This genus is made up of 125 species. The name comes from two Greek words, *gypsos,* meaning "gypsum" or "lime," and *philos,* meaning "loving." This refers to the fact that most species of this genus need alkaline soil, such as comes from gypsum rocks.

The light, airy sprays of pink or white delicate flowers of baby's breath make a wonderful fresh cut flower. They also make outstanding dried flowers. To dry, cut the blooms at their peak and hang them in bunches upside-down in a dark, dry place. An alternative method is to pick the blossoms, put them in a small amount of water, and allow them to dry upright.

COMMON NAME: **balloon flower**
GENUS: *Platycodon*
SPECIES, HYBRIDS, CULTIVARS:
*P. grandiflorum*—single, deep blue
flowers; about 20 inches. *P. g.*
'Album'—white form. *P. g.* 'Shell
Pink'—pink color; best grown in shade.
FAMILY:  Campanulaceae
BLOOMS:  summer
TYPE:  perennial
DESCRIPTION:  Balloon flower has
unique buds that look round and inflated like
a ball or balloon. The flowers, when open,
are bell shaped and come in blue, white, or
pink forms. They are quite long lasting,
starting to bloom in midsummer and lasting
for many weeks. Plants stand approximately
20 inches tall.
CULTIVATION:  Balloon flower needs
sandy, well-drained soil and can be grown in
full sun or partial shade. The pink variety
needs shade because the blossoms tend to
fade in full sun. This plant does not like to
be disturbed after planting. Seeds can be
sown in spring.

Balloon flower creates such beautiful
displays in the Japanese countryside that it is
often mentioned in legends and poems in
that country.

Balloon flower makes a good cut flower. Cut
it late in the afternoon or in early evening
and put the flowers into deep water. The
next day, trim the bottom off each stem and
strip off the lower leaves.

   The genus name comes from two Greek
words, *platys*, meaning "broad," and *kodon*,
meaning "bell," and is descriptive of the
shape of the flower. The common name is
from the shape of the bud, which looks like
a small balloon.

   Also known as Chinese bell flower, this
plant is native to China, where it was used
extensively as a pot herb and for medicine.
The roots were sometimes used as a
substitute for the much-sought-after ginseng
roots.

COMMON NAME: **begonia**
GENUS: *Begonia*
SPECIES, HYBRIDS, CULTIVARS:
*B. semperflorens-cultorum*, glamour series, vision series, varsity series, dwarf hybrids.
FAMILY: Begoniaceae
BLOOMS: summer
TYPE: annual and perennial
DESCRIPTION: Begonias are compact plants with attractive, bright copper green foliage and an abundance of blooms from early summer until frost. Flower colors are pinks, reds, and white.
CULTIVATION: The seeds are tiny—almost dustlike (some species have as many as 100,000 seeds per ounce). They are slow to germinate, so you must plant them indoors two to three months before you place them in the garden. A soil mixture made up of equal parts of soil, sand, and peat moss and constant 70-degree temperatures will give the best conditions for germination. The soil must never be allowed to dry out. European growers cover the fine seeds with a thin layer of small gravel or big sand (you should still be able to see the soil through this layer). This helps to protect the seedlings when you water them, and keeps the moisture even. Once germination has occurred, make sure the seedlings are not exposed to temperatures below 60 degrees Fahrenheit. Feed the plants once a week with a half-strength solution of soluble fertilizer, and provide fourteen to eighteen hours of light per day. Once planted in the garden, begonias will thrive under varying light conditions ranging from partial shade to full sun (with sufficient moisture). They prefer light soil, rich in organic matter. Begonias are actually tender perennials and can be potted up after the summer growing season and brought indoors for the cold months.

Over 1,000 species belong to this genus, and most of these are native to the tropics and subtropics. The entire family was named for Michael Begon, French governor to the West Indies in 1690. An eager amateur botanist, Begon set out, with the help of a French monk, Father Charles Plumier, to collect and identify all the plants in the West Indies. They found many new species, which they sent to the French Academy of Science.

The first begonia had actually been sent to Europe in 1650, but it was considered only a curiosity until Begon began to send many different varieties back from the West Indies. It then gained instant popularity for its colorful foliage and for the fact that it bloomed outdoors in summer and indoors during the winter months.

The discovery of begonias and their subsequent popularity created quite a stir within the botanical world and helped to instigate the creation of further plant exploration teams. In 1777 the governments of both Spain and England sent botanical teams to Central America and South America to look for new plant species.

Begonias were first brought to the United States by Prince Nursery in Long Island, New York, in 1880. The plants soon earned quite a reputation for their beauty and ease of propagation.

Begonias are seldom mentioned in folk tales and superstitions, though a princess wore begonias in her hair in an old Chinese fable. Fourteenth-century minstrels are thought to have used begonias as a symbol of beauty and virtue. This contrasts sharply with the Victorian language of flowers, which considered begonia a symbol of "dark thoughts." The language of tuberous begonias is "dangerous pleasures."

Popular begonias can be divided into three major types: bedding plant begonias, with fibrous roots; houseplant begonias, which grow from rhizomes; and tuberous begonias.

This latter category produces spectacularly colored blossoms and makes a wonderful flowering plant for shady areas. The flowers are large, some measuring as much as 3 to 4 inches across. Tuberous begonias are available in reds, oranges, and pinks and in various flower forms such as carnation or camellia types. The tubers should be planted 1 to 2 inches deep in the spring in an area that gets partial shade. They are quite susceptible to cold, however, and the tubers must be dug and stored in a cool, dry place over the winter.

COMMON NAME: **blanket flower**
GENUS: *Gaillardia*
SPECIES, HYBRIDS, CULTIVARS:
*G. aristata. G. grandiflora*
'Goblin'—perennial; blooms first year from
seed; 12 inches tall. *G.g.* 'Dazzler'—3 feet
tall. *G. pulchella*—annual.
FAMILY: Compositae
BLOOMS: summer
TYPE: perennial and annual
DESCRIPTION: Bright red and yellow
daisy-like flowers appear during the summer.
Many flowers are red with yellow tips. The
center is usually large and dark red, the
leaves light green and lance shaped. Some
varieties produce double flowers.
CULTIVATION: One of the few
perennial garden plants that love the hot sun,
gaillardia can be used in a hot, dry part of
the garden that is unsuitable for other plants.
The plants prefer well-drained, sandy soil of
average fertility. Removing faded blossoms
encourages further bloom. *Crockett's Flower
Garden* suggests that flowers will be more
outstanding if seeds are sown in a nursery
bed in mid-July, overwintered there, and then
moved to a permanent garden location the
following spring. Established plants can be
divided easily in spring.

Gaillardia was named for Gaillard de
Charentonneay, an eighteenth-century
Frenchman who enthusiastically supported
the growing science of botany.

The two species grown most often, *G.
pulchella* and *G. aristata*, are native to
North America and were hybridized in
Belgium in 1857 to form *G. grandiflora*.

The common name is blanket flower, for
it was this plant, growing throughout the
southwestern United States, that inspired
Indian women to include similar designs on
the blankets they wove. One variety is called
Indian chief.

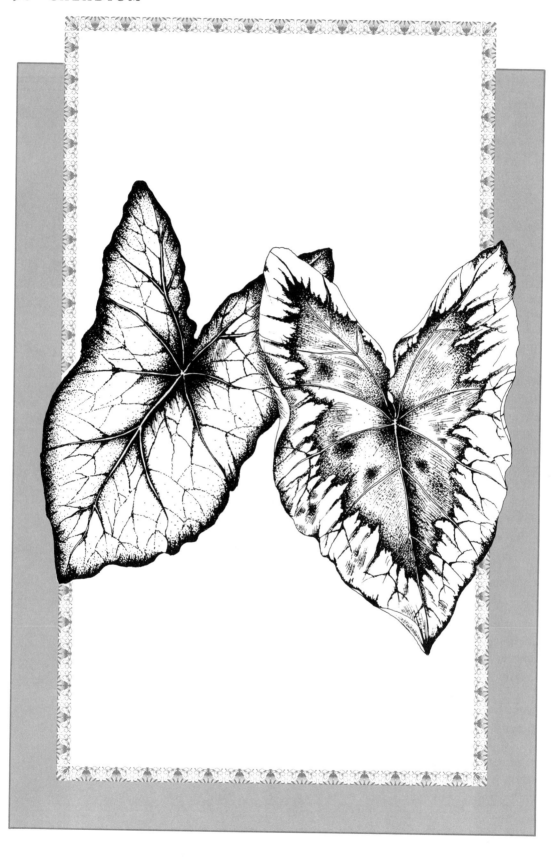

COMMON NAME: caladium
GENUS: *Caladium*
SPECIES, HYBRIDS, CULTIVARS:
*C. bicolor* 'Ivory'—ivory white. *C.b.* 'Little
Miss Muffet'—only 8 to 12 inches tall; wine
red speckles. *C.b.* 'Clarice'—dark green
borders, red veins. *C.b.* 'White Queen'—
18 to 20 inches tall; dark green borders, light
green leaves with red veins.
FAMILY: Araceae
BLOOMS: summer foliage
TYPE: perennial
DESCRIPTION: large, beautifully
colored leaves give caladiums their enviable
loveliness. Foliage colors include shades of
pink, red, white, and green. The leaves have
unusual markings.
CULTIVATION: Caladiums come from
bulbs and are extremely easy to grow. They
prefer lightly shaded areas and rich,
well-drained soil. Plant the bulbs 2 inches
deep once temperatures have warmed. When
the leaves begin to turn brown from fall
frosts, dig up the bulbs and overwinter them
in a cool but not freezing spot. Replant them
in the spring. The plants can also be easily
propagated by taking root cuttings in spring.
Cut the tuber into pieces with at least one
eye each.

———— ❧ ————

This genus comprises fifteen species, all
native to tropical America and the West
Indies.

The most outstanding feature of the
plant is the brightly colored leaves, a result
of successful plant breeding for many years.
The flowers are actually quite small and can
be found crowded onto a spadix (a clublike
spike). Much of the earliest caladium
breeding was done by the French in the late
1800s. The English, Germans, and Brazilians
later took up the work as well, producing
beautifully colored and variegated leaves.

The first notable breeding done in the
United States was performed at the Missouri
Botanical Gardens.

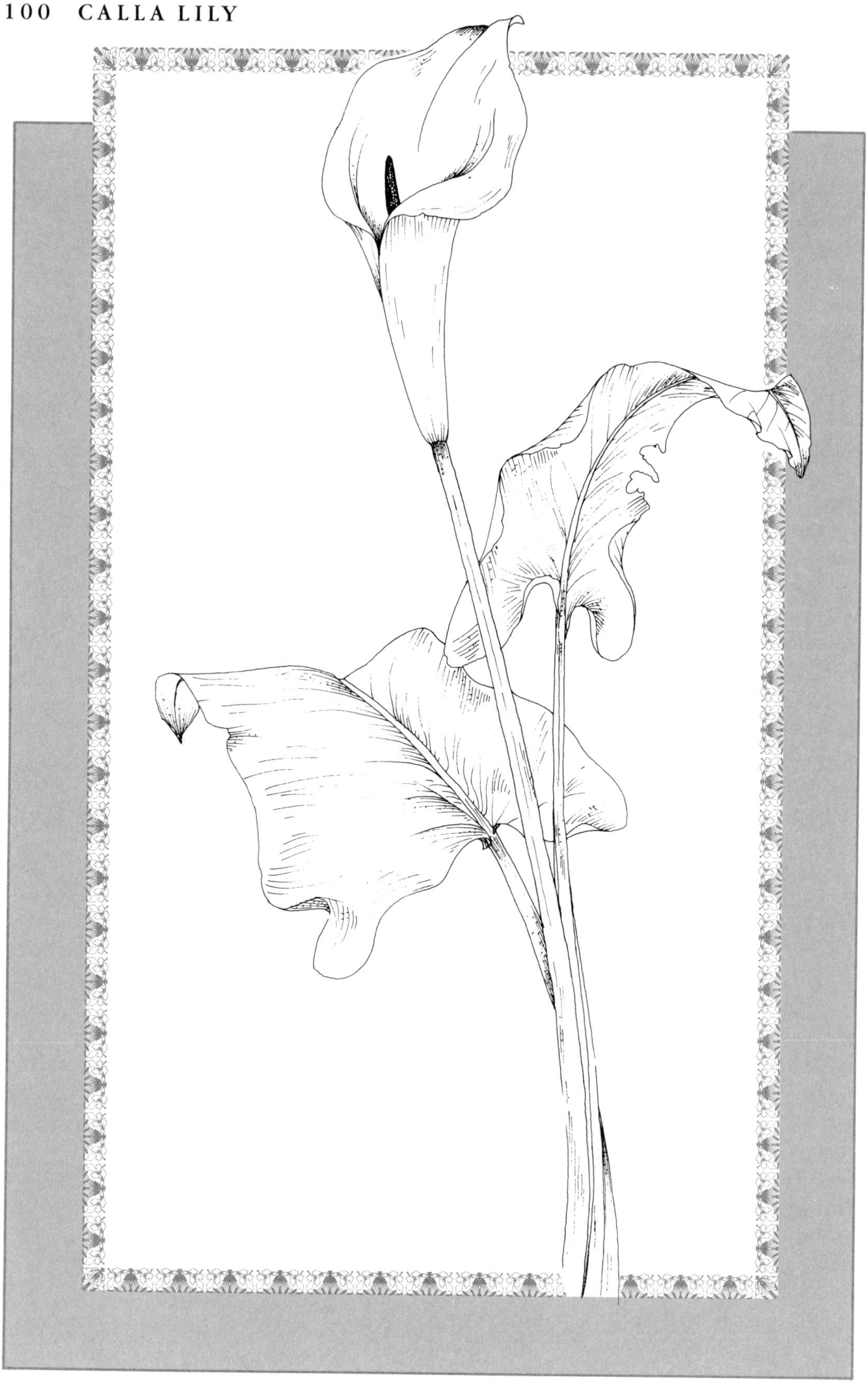

COMMON NAME:   calla lily
GENUS:   *Zantedeschia*
SPECIES, HYBRIDS, CULTIVARS:
*Z. aethiopica*—large; white. *Z. alba-maculata*—dwarf; white with purple blotch at the throat. *Z. elliottiana*—golden flowers; 24 inches; leaves speckled white. *Z. rehmannii*—12 inches, delicate pink.
FAMILY:   Araceae
BLOOMS:   summer
TYPE:   perennial (non-hardy)
DESCRIPTION:   Easily identified by the large trumpet-shaped flower, calla lily is most often found with a white blossom, though shades of yellow and pink are also available. The blossom actually consists of a golden spadix that holds all the flowers and a large, lovely bract (called a spathe) that surrounds the spadix. The leaves are large and arrow shaped.
CULTIVATION:   Calla lilies are often used as a florist's flower or a house plant. The plants like ample watering and will grow even in warm, shallow, not-moving water. In the garden they require rich, moist soil and will benefit from feedings with a complete liquid fertilizer. Warmth is a major requirement of these plants. They will not tolerate any cold. Given the necessary conditions, calla lilies are considered easy to grow.

———— ❧ ————

One of the most beautiful species of this plant from South Africa bears a long and tongue-twisting botanical name, *Zantedeschia aethiopica*. The genus was named for an Italian botanist and physician, Frances Zantedeschi (1773–1846). There are eight species in the genus, all native to South Africa. The species name *aethiopica* is from Ethiopia, for this species was found growing in the upper Nile region. It is also called lily of the Nile.

The name calla is from the Greek word *kalos*, meaning "beautiful." The plant is not only beautiful but is also unusual, for the flowers are clustered tightly along the club, or spadix. The most conspicuous feature of the plant is a single, large, petal-like bract.

COMMON NAME: **canna lily**
GENUS: *Canna*
SPECIES, HYBRIDS, CULTIVARS:
*C. generalis* 'The President'—red; 36 inches.
*C.g.* 'City of Portland'—salmon or pink.
*C.g.* Pfitzer's dwarf varieties—all colors; 18
to 24 inches. *C.g.* 'Nirvana'—red buds open
into yellow blossoms with white stripe.
FAMILY: Cannaceae
BLOOMS: summer–fall
TYPE: perennial
DESCRIPTION: Large, bright, showy
flowers rise above unusually large leaves.
Many, many cultivars boast a wide range of
colors from yellow and orange to red, and
leaf colors from green and bronze to brown.
This adds an exotic look to the summer
garden. Many dwarf varieties are available
now, greatly extending the usefulness of this
plant.
CULTIVATION: Cannas are originally
from the tropics and thrive during long, hot
summers. They will grow well under a
variety of soil conditions, but they appreciate
ample moisture. They are heavy feeders and
benefit greatly from quantities of organic
manure. In late summer or autumn, prepare
cannas for winter by cutting back the stems
to just above soil level and mulching the
plants heavily. In very cold climates the
rhizomes should be lifted and stored over
winter in a warm, dry place. Cannas are
hardy and easy to grow. When setting out
new rhizomes, place them 18 inches apart.

in nut shells and made necklaces of them.
Some of these necklaces were sent back to
Spain during the sixteenth century and were
used as rosary beads.

The common name is from the Latin
word meaning "reed" or "cane" and refers
to the flower scape (flower stalk that rises
directly from the crown at ground level).

---

Canna lily is native to Central America, South
America, Malaysia, and Nepal. The seeds get
very hard and were sometimes called Indian
shot, for they looked like bullets. Some
South American Indian tribes put the seeds

COMMON NAME: cinquefoil
GENUS: *Potentilla*
SPECIES, HYBRIDS, CULTIVARS:
*P. aurea* 'Verna'—trails; 3 inches tall;
May-June; yellow. *P. nepalensis*
'Roxana'—orange red; needs stalking.
*P. thurberi*—native to southwestern United
States; 18 to 24 inches; mahogany red.
FAMILY: Rosaceae
BLOOMS: summer
TYPE: annual and perennial
DESCRIPTION: This genus contains
over 300 species and includes annuals,
perennials, and shrubs. The flowers are
yellow, orange, or red. They look like single
roses and are generally borne in profusion.
The leaves of many species resemble
strawberry leaves.
CULTIVATION: Cinquefoil should be
grown in full sun or light shade. It is not
particular about the acidity of the soil but
does like to be rooted in well-drained, rich
soil. It appreciates regular watering and
generous amounts of organic matter.

Cinquefoil is rich in tannin and has been
used in tanning for centuries. Flowers of
many species grown in Tibet produce tiny,
nutlike roots that are considered delicious
and quite a delicacy. They were also used as
a lure spread on fish nets.

These plants were brought to European
gardens from the Himalayas in the early
1800s.

The fact that plants in this genus were
considered strong medicine is reflected in the
genus name, which is from a Latin word
meaning "powerful." The leaves were made
into a tea used to treat fevers and
inflammations of the mouth and gums. A
solution made from the plant was used as a
gargle and mouth wash and, made into a
poultice, was put on wounds.

Cinquefoil was a favorite ingredient in
witch's brew. Mixed with deadly nightshade,
hemlock, thorn apple, and spiders' legs, this
created a lethal concoction. Witches also
used the plant to produce a trancelike state
by rubbing the leaves over their bodies.

The wild cinquefoil is the symbol of the
beloved daughter, for when it rains the leaves
bend over the flower to protect it from the
rain, as a mother would protect a beloved
daughter.

COMMON NAME:  **clematis**
GENUS:  *Clematis*
SPECIES, HYBRIDS, CULTIVARS:
*C. jackmanii* 'Ramona'—purple. *C.j.*
'Nelly Moser'—pale pink. *C.j.*
*henryi*—white.
*C. maximowicziana*—profusion of white
blossoms late in summer. *C. montana*
*rubens*—rose pink anemone type.
FAMILY:  Ranunculaceae
BLOOMS:  summer
TYPE:  perennial
DESCRIPTION:   Plant breeders have
done marvelous work on this vine, and
cultivars are available in an entire rainbow of
colors from white to pink, red, purples,
blues, and yellows. Flower forms may be
single or double.
CULTIVATION:   Clematis adapts to
many different conditions but prefers its
head in the sun and its feet in the shade—it
likes cool, protected roots but will bloom a
bit better with a little sunshine on the vine.
Sun is more important than shade, for mulch
can be used to protect the roots.

The genus *Clematis* has over 300 species,
most of which are native to eastern Asia, the
Himalayas, and North America.

The genus name is from the Greek word
*klema*, which means "branch of a vine or
climbing plant" and is descriptive of the
growing pattern of the plant.

*C. vitalba*, native to England, grew in
the hedgerows during the time of Roman
occupation and was called traveler's joy
because its sweet fragrance delighted many
foot travelers.

One of the first large species of clematis
introduced for cultivation, *C. lanuginusa*,
was brought from China by nineteenth-
century English botanist Robert Fortune.
Many species are poisonous to the touch,
particularly the young shoots of *C.*

*montana*. Touching this causes a painful rash
and marks that sometimes last for months.

The most famous breeders of clematis
were members of the Jackman family, who
developed the very beautiful hybrid *C.
jackmanii* more than a century ago.

Clematis seems to thrive on occasional
applications of tea, a fact that Peter Coats, a
notable English garden writer, attributes to
their close affinity with British gardeners.

Clematis is a symbol of mental beauty.

COMMON NAME: cleome
GENUS: *Cleome*
SPECIES, HYBRIDS, CULTIVARS:
*C. hasslerana* (often found as *C. spinosa*)
'Helen Campbell'—white. *C.h.* 'Purple
Queen'—lilac purple. *C.h.* 'Pink
Queen'—pink.
*C.h.* 'Cherry Queen'—red.
FAMILY: Capparaceae
BLOOMS: summer
TYPE: annual
DESCRIPTION: Although the flowers
of cleome are very large, measuring 6 to 8
inches across, the plants are so open and airy
that they always look graceful. The plants get
tall, reaching a height of 36 to 48 inches, and
measure 18 to 24 inches across. Because of
cleome's size and quick growth habit, it
should be used in an informal part of the
garden. The leaves are dark green and
attractive but are sticky and thorny. The
flowers have long protruding stamens.
CULTIVATION: Cleome grows well
from seeds and should be sown in the flower
bed in spring. Put cleome in full sun or light
shade, and provide it with average soil. Do
not pinch it back as the seedlings grow.
Frequent watering and applications of liquid
fertilizer will benefit the plants.

There are over 200 species in this genus.
Most are native to tropical or subtropical
regions, but many are indigenous to
temperate parts of the United States.

Cleome is often called spider flower
because of the long, slender stamens that
remind one of spider legs.

If cultivated and allowed to self-sow,
cleomes often revert to a less attractive
species form or color. To prevent reversion,
cut back the flower heads before they go to
seed.

COMMON NAME:    cockscomb
GENUS:    *Celosia*
SPECIES, HYBRIDS, CULTIVARS:
Both tall and dwarf varieties are available.
*C. agentea plumosa*—feathery plumes.
*C.a. cristata*—plume is flattened into fan
shape; often called crested cockscomb.
FAMILY:    Amaranthaceae
BLOOMS:    summer
TYPE:    annual
DESCRIPTION:    Flowers of celosia are
very unusual, producing plumes of reds,
yellows, cream, and orange. Dwarf varieties
are generally 12 inches tall but will spread 9
to 12 inches. Taller varieties will grow to 18
to 24 inches.
CULTIVATION:    Cockscomb grows in
full sun or very light shade in rich, moist
garden soil. Sow seeds directly into the
garden bed or start them indoors at the end
of March. Sow seeds 1/8 inch deep, and thin
taller varieties to 16 inches apart. When
transplanting seedlings, do not plant them
too deeply.

Cockscomb makes a wonderful dried
flower, retaining its color for a long time. To
dry the flowers, cut them at their peak and
hang them upside-down in a dark, dry room.
This plant also makes an outstanding fresh
cut flower.

———— ❧ ————

Most members of this genus are native to the
tropics and are unknown to gardeners. The
species grown most often in our gardens
today, *C. argentea*, is from China. The genus
name is from a Greek word, *kelos*, meaning
"burned," for many species have bright red
flowers that look like a flame.

In Elizabethan England, this member of
the Amaranth family was called floramor or
flower gentle, presumably because it was
considered tender and often was grown only
in a greenhouse.

Because of its exaggerated colors,
cockscomb was considered the symbol of
foppery, affectation, and singularity.

COMMON NAME: coleus
GENUS: *Coleus*
SPECIES, HYBRIDS, CULTIVARS:
*C. hybridus* (sometimes found as
*C. blumei)* 'Candidum'—ivory with green
edges.
*C.h.* 'Chartreuse'—yellow green,
*C.h.* 'Flamenco'—red with yellow edge.
FAMILY: Labiatae
BLOOMS: summer foliage
TYPE: Perennial (usually grown as annual)
DESCRIPTION: Oval, often ruffled,
and lovely colored leaves give coleus its
beauty. Foliage colors include ivory, yellow,
green, and red. Heights of different cultivars
range from 8 to 36 inches, and it spreads to
nearly 12 inches across. The flowers are
small and insignificant.
CULTIVATION: Colors tend to fade in
bright sunlight, so grow these plants in
partial shade. These do best with rich,
fertile, well-drained soil. Plants will benefit
from frequent applications of a fertilizer that
is high in nitrogen. Pinch back young plants
to encourage branching and fuller growth.
Plants can be propagated easily by taking tip
cuttings or from seeds. Seeds can be sown
indoors in early winter (January or
February). Press the seeds into the soil, but
don't cover them for they need light to
germinate. Water them with warm water.
Sow seeds outdoors in late spring.

Although coleus is most often grown for
its outstanding foliage, the flowers of many
species are also quite lovely.

The aromatic leaves of some species are
used as flavoring.

———— ❦ ————

The genus coleus includes nearly 150
species, which grow in warm regions
throughout the world. The genus name is
from the Greek word *koleos*, meaning
"sheath," and refers to the stamens, which
are united into a tube. One of the more
popular species, *C. blumei*, was first found
growing in Java and was named for a Dutch
botanist, Karl L. Blume.

COMMON NAME: **columbine**
GENUS: *Aquilegia*
SPECIES, HYBRIDS, CULTIVARS:
*A. caerulea*—Colorado columbine; sky blue blossoms with white centers; up to 24 inches. *A. canadensis*—red and yellow; 12 to 24 inches. *A. chrysantha*—produces an abundance of yellow flowers; 24 to 30 inches.
FAMILY: Ranunculaceae
BLOOMS: summer
TYPE: perennial
DESCRIPTION: Flowers of the columbine droop and are bell shaped with five long spurs pointing upward. Blossoms come in red and yellow, blue, purple, and many intermediate tones. The foliage is tri-lobed and attractive.
CULTIVATION: Slightly acidic soil rich in humus and good drainage are essential for growing columbines. They do best in light shade but can tolerate full sun except in extremely hot or dry regions. Do not overfertilize, for this results in excessive foliage and reduced flowering. The plants reseed readily. To keep colors pure, deadhead the plants before seeds are set.

The unusual shape of columbine flowers has given rise to numerous common names such as granny's nightcap, blue starry, meeting house (referring to the "heads in a circle" the spurs resembled), and rock bells. The genus name is from the Latin word meaning "eagle," for some thought the floral spurs looked like the claws of an eagle. The name columbine is also from Latin and means "dove," for other people thought that the plant looked like doves' heads.

Columbine is a very ancient plant and was an important medicinal herb during the Middle Ages. In 1373 it was used with seven other herbs as a cure for the "pestilence." It was also thought to be effective in treating measles and smallpox, sore throats, and swollen glands. Taken with saffron, it was used to cure jaundice.

Columbine blossoms were also used as flavoring, and a 1494 banquet menu listed "gely coloured with columbine floures." John Gerard sometimes called it "Herba Leonis," or the "herbe wherein the lion doth delight." This referred to the ancient superstition that lions would eat columbine in the spring to revive their strength.

According to the language of flowers, columbine is the symbol of folly. This was based on the similarity of the shape of the flower to the court jester's cap and bells. It was considered bad luck to give this flower to a woman.

COMMON NAME: (purple) coneflower
GENUS: *Echinacea*
SPECIES, HYBRIDS, CULTIVARS:
*E. purpurea* is one parent (the other parent is unknown) of many hybrids including 'Bright Star'—18 to 24 inches tall; rose red petals with a maroon center. 'Robert Bloom'—carmine flowers with orange center; 24 to 36 inches tall. 'The King' —crimson flowers with maroon brown center; up to 36 inches. 'White Lustre' —white blossoms with golden center; up to 36 inches.
FAMILY: Compositae
BLOOMS: summer
TYPE: perennial
DESCRIPTION: Long-lasting flowers are borne on stiff stems. The petals droop, and the center is raised and covered with stiff spines. The flowers are daisylike. The leaves are large and rough. The spread is generally 12 to 18 inches across.
CULTIVATION: Purple coneflower needs full sun and sandy, well-drained soil. The plants are quite drought tolerant and come very easily from seeds, blooming in two to three years. Purple coneflowers attract Japanese beetles, which could be a problem in areas where these beetles are abundant. For easy propagation, divide the plants in early spring.

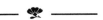

The genus name, *Echinacea*, is from the Greek word for "hedgehog" and refers to the mass of prickly spines on the seed head. Other common names for the plant include droops (because of the way the petals hang downward), red sunflower, and red sunbonnet, for the red tones and the sunflowerlike shape of the blossoms.

Names like Indian root and scurvy root refer to the medicinal value of the plant. It was at one time used extensively as medicine in America, curing such diverse ailments as colds, snakebites, and scurvy.

Modern testing has found chemicals within the plant that are effective in fighting viral infections, including certain venereal diseases and influenza. Also, there is some indication that the plants may be useful in treating certain types of cancers and allergies.

COMMON NAME:  **coral bells**
GENUS:  *Heuchera*
SPECIES, HYBRIDS, CULTIVARS:
*H. sanguinea* 'Bressingham'
hybrids—white, pink, red; grows to 24
inches. *H.s.* 'Chatterbox'—deep rose pink;
18 inches. *H.s.* 'Pluie de Feu'—cherry red;
to 18 inches. *H.s.* *'Rosamundi'*—coral
pink; 18 inches. *H.s.* 'White Cloud'—white
to cream;
18 inches.
FAMILY:  Saxifragaceae
BLOOMS:  summer
TYPE:  perennial
DESCRIPTION:  Coral bells is a graceful
perennial that is good for borders and rock
gardens. Growing to a height of 18 inches,
this compactly mounding plant spreads
approximately 12 to 18 inches. The leaves
are lobed and evergreen. The flowers occur
on panicles (irregularly branched flower
clusters) and rise above the leaves.
CULTIVATION:  Coral bells need
well-drained soil, rich in organic matter.
Plant them 12 inches apart in spring, placing
the crowns 1 inch below the soil. The plants
will grow in full sun or partial shade and
should be mulched in northern areas after
the ground has frozen. Seeds can be sown
outdoors in early May for blooms the
following summer. Propagation can also be
accomplished by dividing plants in spring.

the blossoms. The species name *sanguinea* is
from the Latin word meaning "bloody" or
"blood red" and refers to the color of the
blossom. Other common names include
matin bells and alum root.

———— ❧ ————

Over fifty species of *Heuchera* are native to
North America. Most people consider the
hybrids much more beautiful than the native
species.

The genus was named for Johann
Heinrich von Heucher, a German botanist
and professor of medicine who died in 1747.

The common name coral bells is
descriptive of the color and configuration of

COMMON NAME: coreopsis

GENUS: *Coreopsis*

SPECIES, HYBRIDS, CULTIVARS:
*C. auriculata. C. lanceolata*
'Sunburst'—semi-double; yellow; to 24
inches. *C.l.* 'Mayfield Giant'—yellow; to 36
inches. *C.l.* 'New Gold'—double yellow
flowers; up to 30 inches. *C. verticillata*
'Golden Shower'—yellow; to 24 inches.
*C.v.* 'Zagreb'—blooms July–frost; single
yellow flowers; up to 12 inches.
*C. grandiflora* 'Goldfink'—deep yellow
flowers; 2 to 3 inches across; blooms early
June–frost; up to 9 inches tall. *C.g.*
'Sunray'—double flowers; up to 20 inches
tall; heat and drought tolerant.

FAMILY: Compositae

BLOOMS: summer

TYPE: annual and perennial

DESCRIPTION: *C. verticillata* is
considered one of the best perennials
available to the home gardener. It is easy to
grow and generally pest-free, and it produces
clear lemon yellow flowers over a long
time—from June until September. The leaves
are threadlike and remain attractive
throughout the growing season.
*C. lanceolata* has broader leaves and has
been hybridized to give us both single and
double forms. Both species reach a height of
between 12 and 36 inches and spreads of 12
to 24 inches.

CULTIVATION: Coreopsis is a native
American wildflower found growing in fields
and other open places, indicating its need for
full sun. Though it does not need
particularly fertile soil, coreopsis will
perform best in soils that are sandy and well
drained. All varieties will grow easily from
seed. *C. lanceolata* and its hybrids seldom
need dividing. *C. verticillata* should be
divided every three to four years in spring.
This species is quite drought tolerant.

Coreopsis has been called the plant with the
sunny disposition. The genus name is from
Latin and means "bed bug," because the
seeds are black, have a small hook on one
end, and look like small bugs. Another
common name is tickseed, for some people
thought the seeds looked like ticks rather
than bed bugs. Pioneers used seeds from the
plant stuffed in pillows and mattresses to
help repel insects.

All members of the genus *Coreopsis* are
native to North America, but they are not
among the first plants introduced to
European gardeners from the New World.
The first species to be included within
English gardens was *C. auriculata*, which
appeared in 1699. It was not until 100 years
later that the annual species, *C. tinctoria*,
was introduced, but once it arrived, it
became extremely popular. The species name
*tinctoria* means "of the dyers," or "of dyes,"
and refers to the practice of using this plant
to dye cloth red.

Coreopsis makes a very good,
long-lasting cut flower.

COMMON NAME: **cornflower**

GENUS: *Centaurea*

SPECIES, HYBRIDS, CULTIVARS:
*C. cyanus* 'Polka Dot'—mixture of white, rose pink, and blue. *C.c.* 'Jubilee Gem'—dwarf; double blue flowers. *C.c.* 'Dwarf Snowball'—white form.

FAMILY: Compositae

BLOOMS: summer

TYPE: annual

DESCRIPTION: Standard height of the cornflower is 24 to 36 inches; dwarf strains are usually 12 to 15 inches tall. These are delicate, airy plants with small foliage and an abundance of flowers that are 1/2 to 2 inches across. Taller varieties tend to flop over and may need staking.

CULTIVATION: The flowers last only three to four weeks, but deadheading can extend the blooming period. Mildew can be a problem, so grow cornflowers in a sunny, open area. They grow well in average soil and will tolerate drought conditions fairly well. Seeds can be sown in spring (around April 1) or fall. Sow seeds 1/4 inch deep, and thin plants to 8 inches apart.

This genus was named for the centaur Chiron, who was wounded by an arrow poisoned with the blood of Hydra, the nine-headed serpent. He used blossoms of cornflower to dress the wound, and this gave the flower both its healing powers and its name.

The species name came from a mythical youth, Cyanus, who loved flowers so much that he spent all his time wandering through the fields making wreaths from the flowers. His favorite of all flowers was the cornflower. When he died, Cyanus was found in a bed of blue cornflowers. Flora, goddess of flowers, was so touched by his devotion that she turned him into his favorite flower.

The common name cornflower is from England, where this plant often comes up in fields of grain. A very ancient belief was that in years of bad luck, cornflowers instead of grain would come from the seeds sown in spring.

During medieval times this plant was sometimes called hurt sickle. Ancient harvesting tools were often flimsy and, though they easily cut through the fine stalks of grain, they could not cut through cornflower's stouter stalks, and the blades were sometimes damaged.

Medicinal use of cornflower was limited, but it was thought to be good for nervous disorders and was used as an eyewash to improve eyesight. Certain types of paralysis (such as that resulting from a stroke) were thought to be improved by the flower. The blossoms, boiled in beer, were also used to treat jaundice.

Pigment from the flowers was said to turn sugar a strange, but beautiful color, and was also used to make paint.

When Queen Louise of Prussia was forced by Napoleon to flee from Berlin, she hid her children in a cornfield and kept them entertained and quiet by weaving wreaths of cornflowers. One of these children, Wilheim, years later became emperor of Germany. Remembering his mother's bravery, he made the cornflower a national emblem of unity.

Cornflowers have been grown in English gardens for many years. Records show that many colors were grown as early as 1629. According to the language of flowers, cornflower is a symbol of delicacy.

COMMON NAME: cosmos
GENUS: *Cosmos*
SPECIES, HYBRIDS, CULTIVARS:
*C. sulphureus* 'Diablo'—bright orange red
or yellow flowers; 24 to 30 inches tall.
*C. bipinnatus*—tall; feathery leaves; large,
2- to 3-inch pink and white flowers.
FAMILY: Compositae
BLOOMS: summer
TYPE: annual
DESCRIPTION: Airy and delicate,
cosmos adds nice texture as well as color to
the summer garden. The leaves are finely
dissected, the blossoms daisylike. Double
cultivars are available, though many people
like the old-fashioned charm of the single
blossoms.
CULTIVATION: Cosmos comes from
seed very easily. Sow it in late spring, and
blooms will appear in eight to ten weeks.
Cosmos needs full or half-day sun and
thrives in good, rich garden soil, though it
adapts to less fertile conditions. Once the
seedlings are established, they can withstand
long periods of drought.

Spanish plant collectors first found
cosmos growing in Mexico. Seeds from the
plant were taken back to Spain and from
there were taken to England. Cosmos was
not grown commercially until the mid 1800s.

The word cosmos is from the Greek
word meaning "ordered universe" and was
given to this plant because of the simple
balance of the blossoms. Spanish priests were
said to have grown it in their gardens as a
symbol of harmony.

Cosmos is the floral emblem for the
month of October.

———— ✿ ————

In 1897 the Plant Introduction Center in
Washington, D.C., was looking for new plant
species of horticultural value that could
adapt easily to different climates in the
United States. One of the flowers that caught
their eye was cosmos, a native of Mexico.
They found that the hardy little cosmos was
tolerant of hot, dry conditions and was very
suitable for growing in the southwestern part
of the United States. Since that time, cosmos
has been grown in gardens all over the
country. Because it adapts to varied cultural
conditions and reseeds easily, it is also
desirable for naturalizing in a meadow. It is
particularly good for attracting
hummingbirds and butterflies.

COMMON NAME:   dahlia
GENUS:   *Dahlia*
SPECIES, HYBRIDS, CULTIVARS:
Anemone forms: *D.* 'Fable'—scarlet;
30 inches. *D.* 'Honey'—apricot and pink;
30 inches. *D.* 'San Luis Rey'—pink; 48
inches. Cactus forms: *D.* 'Gold
Crown'—bronze yellow. *D.* 'Brookside
Cheri'—salmon pink; 48 to 60 inches.
*D.* 'Park Jewel'—dark pink; 24 inches.
FAMILY:   Compositae
BLOOMS:   summer
TYPE:   perennial (tender)
DESCRIPTION:   Several types of dahlias
include anemone forms, with softly cupped
and rounded petals, and cactus forms, which
have long, narrow spinelike petals. Colors
include yellow, orange, red, white, cream,
and pink.
CULTIVATION:   Dahlias need full sun or
very light shade and ample watering during
dry summer months. Rich topsoil will
benefit the plants. They are heavy feeders,
and the leaves will turn yellow with
insufficient nutrients. Tubers should be
planted at a depth of 6 inches in spring after
all danger of frost has passed. After the first
fall frost, dig up the tubers, allow them to
dry in the sun a few hours, then store them
in slightly damp sand in a plastic bag in a
cool place where temperatures do not get
below 35 to 40 degrees Fahrenheit.

It has been estimated that more than 3,000
varieties of dahlias are available.

No one really knows how long these
magnificent flowers have been cultivated, for
they were found in Mexican gardens when
the Spanish arrived. An Aztec herbal written
in the early sixteenth century lists
cocoxochitl (as dahlias were then called) as a
cure for epilepsy. The plant tuber is large and
fleshy, contains high amounts of fructose,
and is quite nutritious. The tubers were used
for food in Central America, South America,
and Mexico.

When cocoxochitl was sent to Spain
from Mexico, its beauty created quite a
sensation. In 1789 the king of Spain changed
the name of the flower to dahlia, in honor of
Anders Dahl, a Swedish botanist who created
many new hybrids. The king of Spain then
declared a day of celebration in honor of
Spain's claim to this marvelous new flower.
He also proclaimed that any other country
possessing this flower did so illegally, since
Mexico, its place of origin, was a province of
Spain.

The desirability of the flower
superseded any royal proclamation, however,
and dahlias were soon growing in many
other countries. One story tells of a Dutch
plant breeder who asked a Mexican friend to
send him a box of dahlia tubers. When they
arrived only one of the tubers was still alive,
but this proved to be a lovely new strain and
was crossed with other hybrids to form the
first of the modern dahlias.

Many English gardeners had a difficult
time getting dahlias established, and for this
reason, dahlias became the symbol of
instability. In spite of this, by 1829, dahlias
were considered the most fashionable flower
in England.

By the 1830s, dahlias were extremely
popular throughout Europe and mild
"dahliamania" set in. Prices rose
astronomically, and soon the market was
saturated. They were used extensively in
plantings in parks and other public places.

Because of the high sugar content in the
roots, dahlias were sometimes used
medicinally. Before insulin was discovered,
diabetics were given injections of "diabetic
sugar" made from dahlia tubers. Chemicals
from the tubers were also used to make
a solution used to test for kidney disease,
insulin, and levolose, used to test for liver
problems. Alice Coats in her book *Flowers*

*and Their Histories* says that three tons of surplus dahlia roots are used for medicinal purposes annually.

Yellow dahlias, used as a dye, will turn wool a deep rust color. If the wool is put through a second dye bath, the color will turn to light orange.

The petals can be eaten raw, chopped up in salads.

COMMON NAME: **daisy**
GENUS: *Chrysanthemum*
SPECIES, HYBRIDS, CULTIVARS:
*C. leucanthemum*—species daisy; common along roadsides and in fields; single, white.
*C. maximum* 'Polaris'—tall Shasta.
*C.m.* 'Little Miss Muffet'—short Shasta.
*C.m.* 'Esther Read'—double white.
FAMILY: Compositae
BLOOMS: summer
TYPE: perennial
DESCRIPTION: Bright yellow centers and stark white ray flowers make daisies a crisp and beautiful part of the garden. Short and tall forms are available, ranging in height from 12 to 24 inches. There are both single and double forms.
CULTIVATION: Daisies like a lot of sun, though the double forms might appreciate a bit of shady protection from the heat of the afternoon sun. The hybrids like rich, well-drained soil with plenty of moisture. The species form grows quite easily from seed, thrives in poor to average soil, and is tolerant of drought conditions. Plants of both the species and hybrid forms can be divided in spring or fall.

———— ✿ ————

The common name daisy comes from "day's eye" and was mentioned by such early writers as Chaucer. According to the doctrine of signatures, daisies were used to cure eye problems. The English had a multitude of names for the daisy including moondaisy, moon flower, or thunder flower (because it was thought to have the powers to guard one against thunder and lightning). It was also called Saint John's flower, and bruisewort, since the flowers, mixed with water, were used to treat bruised skin. The German name for the flower is *ganesblume*, or goose flower, presumably for the color of the petals. In Yorkshire it is called bairnwort, or "beloved by children." In Sweden it is known as *prastkrage*, or "priest's collar," because the bright white petals of daisies were similar to the starched white collars worn by Lutheran priests.

The blossoms were boiled in water, and the resulting solution was good for chapped and rough skin. The flower, pounded into a powder and mixed with wine, was thought to be an effective tonic. The flowers were also thought to hold the powers to remove warts and cure insanity.

Superstitions connected with the daisy abound. The best known of these is the fortune-telling powers of the blossom. If one were to pick a blossom and then pluck off the petals one by one and chant "he loves me" with the first and "he loves me not" with the next, and so on, the last petal left would tell whether one was loved or not. When an English milkmaid wanted to dream of her lover, she would put her shoes outside the door and daisy roots under her pillow.

To eat the daisy roots was said to stunt your growth. The roots were sometimes fed to puppies in the hope that they would stay small lap dogs. To dream of daisies in spring was thought to bring months of good luck, but to dream of daisies in fall was considered very bad luck.

An ancient Celtic legend says that daisies appeared from the spirits of children who died at birth. God sprinkled these bright and lovely flowers across the earth to cheer the grieving parents.

Daisy is the flower of April, and according to the Victorian language of flowers, is the symbol of innocence.

COMMON NAME: **day lily**
GENUS: *Hemerocallis*
SPECIES, HYBRIDS, CULTIVARS:
*H. fulva*—orange. *H. Lilioasphodelus*
—yellow. Countless varieties are available in a wide range of colors and blooming times from May to September. Dwarf varieties are also available. Tetraploid hybrids are artificially created genetic mutants that produce more flowers in vivid colors, more stem, and more foliage. Some consider them less graceful than the diploid varieties.
FAMILY: Liliaceae
BLOOMS: summer
TYPE: perennial
DESCRIPTION: Large lily flowers are borne several to a stem. Each blossom lasts only a single day, but such a profusion of blossoms appears on the stems that they are attractive for a long time. The foliage is dark green, long, and narrow. Generally day lilies grow 2 to 4 feet tall.
CULTIVATION: Day lilies are quite tough and adaptable. They can be moved just about anytime and like full sun (although some of the paler colors need a bit of shade). Their roots are hardy and vigorous, and the plants appreciate fertilizer in late winter or very early spring. Choose a 5-10-10 fertilizer, for excessive amounts of nitrogen make the stems weak. Plants will need dividing every three to five years. Small divisions can be set out in spring, 1 foot apart.

The day lilies that we grow and cherish today were originally grown in the fields of central China and were cultivated, not for their beauty, but for their wonderfully delicate flavor. The buds were eaten as a spring tonic and any extra buds were dried to be enjoyed during the winter months. Not only were day lilies tasty, they were also good for you, holding such diverse powers as the ability to relieve pain, cure kidney ailments, and lessen grief. It was called *hsuan t'sao*, "the plant of forgetfulness," and was said to cure sorrow by causing a loss of memory. Day lily was also thought to have the power to cause the birth of a son, if it was "worn in the girdle of one's gown during pregnancy," according to a Chinese herbal. The leaves were also used to treat burns and as cattle feed.

Day lilies made their way westward in caravans that followed the Oriental silk routes to eastern Europe. They were brought to England in the late sixteenth century by French Huguenot refugees from France and made their way to the United States by way of Dutch settlers in Manhattan.

The genus name, *Hemerocallis*, is from two Greek words meaning "the beauty of a day."

Day lilies are grown today for their beauty and make a quite desirable garden plants. They are, however, just as edible today as they were thousands of years ago, though some of the flavor might have been lost through extensive breeding. The blossoms can be stuffed with chicken or shrimp salad for an unusually beautiful summer luncheon, or the buds can be used fresh or dried and can be added to soups, meat, or pasta dishes.

COMMON NAME: **delphinium**
GENUS: *Delphinium*
SPECIES, HYBRIDS, CULTIVARS:
*D. chinensis*—low growing; treat as biennial; Pacific Coast hybrids are large, 84 to 96 inches tall. *D. belladonna*—light blue; 60 inches tall. *D. bellamosa*—dark blue; 48 inches tall; Blackmore and Langdon strains; blues, whites, creams, also dwarf forms.
FAMILY: Ranunculaceae
BLOOMS: summer
TYPE: perennial
DESCRIPTION: Called the "queen of garden plants," delphinium should be the high point of the perennial bed, both figuratively and literally. Delphiniums get quite tall and bear very large and beautiful spikes of flowers in shades of blues and lavenders, white, and cream.
CULTIVATION: Delphiniums take a lot of effort, but the rewards are worth the work involved. The flower spike is so big, it needs protection from wind and rain. It also needs full sun and rich, light soil, very high in fertility. To prepare a site for delphinium, pour in compost or rotted manure and a 5-10-10 fertilizer. Water the site thoroughly and allow it to settle several weeks before planting. A bed can be prepared in fall for a spring planting. The plants will need staking, so prepare for this as the buds appear. To encourage a second blooming period, cut back the flowering stalks, but never cut their leaves.

The shape of the blossom suggested both the common and botanical names for this plant. Delphinium is from Greek words meaning "dolphin," for the long spur of the flower reminded some people of the nose of a dolphin. This spur also suggested names like larkspur, lark's heel, or lark's claw. The species *D. ajacis* originated, according to legend, during the ancient battle at Troy. Here the warrior Achilles was slain, and his mother asked that her son's armor be given to the most heroic Greek warrior. Although the brave Ajax expected to be chosen, the armor was given to Ulysses, and in his disappointment, Ajax killed himself. Where his blood spilled is where the small blue larkspur began to grow.

Delphinium is native to China, Siberia, Europe, and North America, and wherever it grows, it has been used as strong external medicine. The most ancient use is to drive away scorpions and other beasts; the seeds and leaves are supposedly so powerful that the beasts are made powerless. The seeds, ground into a powder, were used for a toothache. Many species were used as an insecticide to destroy lice in hair. Larkspur was used for this purpose at both the Battle of Waterloo and during the American Civil War. *D. consolida* was also used to dress wounds. The species name means "to consolidate" or "to close together." The plants are extremely poisonous, and the wild strains are often the cause of death among cattle.

This is the flower for July and, according to the Victorian lanaguage of flowers, is a symbol for swiftness and lightness.

COMMON NAME: **flax**
GENUS: *Linum*
SPECIES, HYBRIDS, CULTIVARS:
*L. flavum*—yellow; 15 inches tall; June. *L. perenne*—sky blue; 12 to 18 inches tall.
*L.p.* 'Album'—white. All the preceeding forms are perennial.
*L. grandiflorum rubrum*—annual; red; reseeds easily.
FAMILY: Linaceae
BLOOMS: summer
TYPE: perennial and annual
DESCRIPTION: Flax is a very airy and delicate-looking plant. The stems are wiry, the leaves long and slender. Flowers come in blue, white, and red, and plants grow 15 to 18 inches tall. Flowers last only a single day and are not suitable for cutting.
CULTIVATION: Flax comes easily from seed—particularly the annual variety. Sow seeds in May and then again three to four weeks later to extend the blooming period. Use flax in the rock garden or in clumps. Perennial flax can also be grown from seeds sown in mid-July, protected over the winter, and set out the following spring. Perennial species are easily propagated by stem cuttings. Plant both perennial and annual species in full sun in well-drained soil. Because the plants look so delicate, they will show best in front of the border.

Flax is probably one of the first non-food plants ever cultivated. For many centuries flax has been prized for its fibers, which are made into linen cloth. According to the Reader's Digest book *Magic and Medicine of Plants*, archaeologists have found flax fibers dating back to prehistoric lake dwellers who lived in Switzerland nearly 10,000 years ago.

The annual flax, *L. usitatissimum*, is most often used for its fibers. The species name is from Latin and means "most useful of the linen family."

To make cloth, flax plants are cut when they are about 3 feet tall, and the stems are soaked in water for several days. The bark is discarded, and the stems are crushed and beaten to separate the fibers, which are then spun into cloth.

White linen was considered a symbol of purity and was often worn by ancient priests. Throughout many centuries, linen was a precious commodity and a measure of one's wealth.

Flax has other uses as well. The flowers were held to be important for their ability to protect against witchcraft. The seeds have been used in medicine to make liniment, cough syrups, and poultices for burns and skin irritations. The seeds have also been used to make linoleum, linseed oil (a drying agent in paints), and oilcloth. The oil is used in cattle feed.

Fibers of the plant were being used to make paper in A.D. 750 in the Moslem Empire. The name flax is from a Latin word meaning "flailing," referring to beating the fibers so they can be separated.

According to the Victorian language of flowers, flax is a symbol of industry.

COMMON NAME:  **flowering tobacco**
GENUS:  *Nicotiana*
SPECIES:  *N. alata. N. affinis*—pure white.
FAMILY:  Solanaceae
BLOOMS:  summer
TYPE:  annual
DESCRIPTION:  Flowering tobacco has attractive, five-petaled, trumpet-shaped flowers that are crimson, white, pink, lime green, or purple. The fragrance from the blossoms is strong and sweet. Plants get approximately 12 to 14 inches tall, and blossoms are 2 to 2 ¹/₂ inches across. The flowers of most species open in the evening or on cloudy days, though new strains that stay open all day have been developed.
CULTIVATION:  Seeds can be started indoors six to eight weeks before setting the plants out in the garden. Seeds can also be sown directly into flower beds once the soil has warmed. The seeds need light to germinate, so do not cover them. Blossoms generally appear on the plants in six weeks from seed. Give plants rich, moist soil and full sun and they will reward you with a profusion of flowers.

Flowering tobacco is in the same family as the plant that supplies tobacco for cigars, cigarettes, snuff, and so on. Although it attracted much attention and great attempts were made to make it economically important, flowering tobbaco has no value except in the garden.

It was first found growing in South America in Brazil, Uruguay, and Paraguay. The genus was named for Jean Nicot, a French consul to Portugal who introduced tobacco to the royal courts of Portugal and France.

Nicotiana's lovely flowers make good, fragrant cut flowers. This plant can be grown in pots and brought indoors for further enjoyment.

COMMON NAME: **forget-me-not**
GENUS: *Myosotis*
SPECIES, HYBRIDS, CULTIVARS:
*M. scorpioides semperflorens*—prostrate
form. *M. alpestris* 'Victoria'—forms
mounds 6 to 8 inches tall; biennial.
FAMILY: **Boraginaceae**
BLOOMS: summer
TYPE: perennial and biennial
DESCRIPTION: Dainty blue flowers
with yellow eyes form neat, low-growing
mounds. The foliage is bright green, glossy,
and attractive. The plants reach a height of
18 inches and are good for massing among
spring bulbs or in the front of the border.
CULTIVATION: Rich, moist soil and
partial sun are the best cultural conditions
for perennial forget-me-not. Plants can be
divided in summer. This is a wonderful plant
to use as a woodland ground cover.

Forget-me-not grows in many countries
throughout the world. According to legend,
this is because of an angel who fell in love
with a mortal woman. He was exiled from
heaven and was told that he could return
only if he placed forget-me-not in every
corner of the world. His beloved agreed to
help him, and together they took sprigs of
forget-me-not throughout the world. Saint
Peter was so moved by their love and
devotion to one another that he allowed
them both to enter heaven.

Several other legends tell of the origin of
this flower. One says that after the earth was
created, God went to each plant and animal
and gave each a name. As God finished and
was getting ready to leave, he heard a little
voice at his feet saying "what about me?" He
bent down and picked up the little plant
whom he had forgotten, and said, "Because I
forgot once, I shall never forget you again,
and that shall be your name."

Another story about the origin of the
name does not have such a happy ending. A
couple in love were walking through the
mountains. The woman saw this small blue
flower growing on a steep hillside and
begged her lover to get it. He climbed to it
but then slipped and fell to his death, tossing
her the flower and calling "forget me not."

Another suggestion as to the origin of
the name is that the leaves taste so bad, once
you have eaten them, you will never forget
them.

Princess Grace of Monaco was a great
flower lover, and she told this story of
forget-me-not: Two men were bragging about
their dogs, each declaring that his was the
smartest. One man finally ended the
discussion by declaring that if he forgot to
feed his dog, the dog would bring him a
sprig of forget-me-not!

Another name for the plant is scorpion
grass, presumably given because the
flowering stalks coil tightly before they
bloom, looking somewhat like a scorpion's
tail. Based on the doctrine of signatures, the
plant was used to cure the bite of spiders and
scorpions. Mixed with oil and wax,
forget-me-not was made into a poultice used
to treat insect bites. In Siberia, it was used to
treat syphilis.

Egyptian healers believed that if you
placed the leaves of this plant over your eyes
during certain times of the year, you would
have visions. The flower was considered
sacred to the Egyptian god Thoth, god of
wisdom.

In the Victorian language of flowers,
forget-me-not means friendship, loving
remembrance, and fidelity.

Forget-me-not is the Alaskan state
flower.

COMMON NAME: **four-o'clock**
GENUS: *Mirabilis*
SPECIES, HYBRIDS, CULTIVARS:
*M. jalapa* 'Jingles'—striped flowers.
*M.j.* *'Pygmy'*—18 inches tall.
*M.j.* *'Petticoat'*—flower-within-flower effect.
FAMILY: Nyctaginaceae
BLOOMS: summer
TYPE: perennial (tender)
DESCRIPTION: Brightly colored, trumpet-shaped flowers open in late afternoon and stay open until the next morning. The plants grow to a height of 48 inches and spread 12 to 24 inches across. Flowers occur in white, lavender, pink, yellow, and salmon.
CULTIVATION: Four-o'clocks need bright, full sun and well-drained soil. The tuber may be dug and stored over winter (as dahlias are done). They grow very quickly and make a good low hedge. Four-o'clocks have the added advantage of being able to withstand air pollution.

Four-o'clocks were named for their unusual blooming habits. The plants generally do not open until late afternoon, or even later. The French call it *belle de nuit*, and the Italians, *bella di notte*. They produce a fragrance that is particularly pleasing to night-flying moths.

The genus was at one time known as *Admiralis*, but Carolus Linnaeus changed it to *Mirabilis*, meaning "admirable or wonderful."

Four-o'clocks, also known as marvel of Peru, have been grown in European gardens since 1540 and were so easy to cultivate that some considered them weeds.

The seeds, beaten or ground into a powder, were used by the Japanese for making cosmetics. The Chinese soaked the blossoms in water to extract the pigment and then used this dye to color gelatin made from seaweed.

The family name is from two Greek words, meaning "night blooming," and describes the growth habits of many species in the family.

The Colorado four-o'clock is native to North America and grows in high elevations in sandy soils. The roots, which have something of a peppery taste, have been used as an appetite suppresser. Hopi Indians chewed the roots to induce a trancelike state.

COMMON NAME:  foxglove
GENUS:  *Digitalis*
SPECIES, HYBRIDS, CULTIVARS:
*D. mertonensis (grandiflora* x
*purpurea)*—perennial; flowers the color of
crushed strawberries. *D. purpurea* 'Giant
Shirley'—biennial; reseeds; large bell-shaped
blossoms in white, pink, rose dotted with
brown, or crimson. *D.p.* 'Alba'—up to 48
inches tall; biennial; white. *D.p.*
'Foxy'—blooms in five months from seed.
FAMILY:  *Scrophulariaceae*
BLOOMS:  summer
TYPE:  perennial and biennial
DESCRIPTION:  Tall spires of gently
colored, bell-shaped flowers make foxglove a
favorite garden plant. Most varieties grow to
a height of 36 to 48 inches, providing a
marvelous backdrop for smaller flowering
plants. Blossoms open progressively up the
stem and create a pyramid effect with the
large, open flowers at the bottom and small,
tight buds at the top.
CULTIVATION:  Foxglove needs partial
shade and rich, well-drained soil with plenty
of moisture. Sow seeds in May, but do not
expect bloom until the following summer.
Do not cover seeds when sowing, for they
need light for germination. Mulch during
winter to protect the roots.

A multitude of common names (some say as
many as sixty-five) have been used to refer to
foxglove. Both the unusual shape of the
blossoms and the potent medicinal properties
of the plant have given rise to many of these
names.

The name foxglove probably developed
from the words "folk's glove." Folks refers to
the little people, or fairies. One possible
origin for this name is a legend about fairies
who gave the blossoms to foxes to wear as
gloves so they would not get caught raiding
the chicken coop.

Another possible origin for the name is
from fox's glew, a glew being an ancient
English musical instrument. The bell shape of
the flower, perhaps, reminded some of this
instrument.

In Cheshire the name is fairy's
petticoats, and in Ireland, fairy's cap. The
French call it *gants de Notre Dame*, Our
Lady's gloves, or *doigts de la Vierge*, the
Virgin's finger. Ancient Druids considered
this their own flower, claiming that each
blossom looked like a Druid hat.

Chemicals from the plant have been
used for medicine for many centuries, but
taken in incorrect amounts, they can be
extremely poisonous. The poisonous
properties have been the cause of names like
bloody fingers, deadman's bells, witch's
thimble, and bloody bells.

According to ancient superstition, if you
picked foxglove, you would offend the
fairies. And if the fairies stole your baby, the
juice of foxglove would help to get it back.

Foxglove was apparently not used as
medicine by ancient Greeks or Romans or
during the medieval period. First record of it
being used as a folk medicine was in 1775
when Dr. William Withering, a Shropshire
physician, noticed the wonderful results
obtained by herb women who used the
plant. Dr. Withering collected foxglove and
painstakingly experimented with it,
discovering the correct amounts needed to
heal. He eventually married a young woman
who had long suffered from heart disease
and whom he was able to heal with
foxglove.

Herb healers had used the powers of
foxglove for many years to treat problems of
the heart. It was believed, however, that the
plant held medicinal power only if it was
collected with the left hand.

Digitalin, a chemical found in the leaves
of foxglove, has been used extensively to

treat heart disease. Experiments are being conducted to develop new strains of foxglove with concentrated amounts of this chemical.

Foxglove has also been used externally. Poultices and compresses using foxglove were thought to be helpful in treating headaches and inflammations.

In northern Wales, a dye from the blossoms was used to color stonework. In Kent, foxglove stalks were used to make parasol handles.

Foxglove thrives in soil that is rich in iron and coal. In the Soviet Union, new coal fields were sometimes located from the air by finding masses of foxglove growing together.

The language of foxglove is insincerity, since it can sometimes heal and sometimes hurt a patient.

COMMON NAME:  **fuchsia**
GENUS:  *Fuchsia*
SPECIES, HYBRIDS, CULTIVARS:
Hybrids have been developed from
*F. magellanica* and *F. fulgens*. *F.* 'Flying
Cloud'—white. *F.* 'South Gate'—large,
double pink. *F.* 'Swing Time'—double white
corolla, red sepals. *F.* 'Voodoo'—very large,
double purple with crimson sepals.
FAMILY:  *Onagraceae*
BLOOMS:  summer
TYPE:  perennial (tender)
DESCRIPTION:  Fuchsia produces
magnificent drooping sprays of nodding
flowers and makes a perfect hanging basket
plant. Flower colors include white, pink, red,
and purple.
CULTIVATION:  Fuchsia is hardy
outdoors in very few areas, but it is
wonderful potted in containers or hanging
baskets. The best potting mixture is
composed of mostly potting soil with a bit
of coarse sand, leaf mold, and bone meal.
Pot up the plants into a clay container that
has been soaking in water. Fuchsias will need
a great deal of attention during the growing
season. The soil must be kept damp, but not
wet, necessitating light but frequent watering
and frequent applications of liquid fertilizer.
Fuchsias are somewhat intolerant of extreme
heat or cold and do best with warm days
and cool nights.

Fuchsia, also known as lady's eardrops,
was named for Leonard Fuchs, a sixteenth-
century German botanist and professor of
medicine.

*F. magellanica*, a scarlet and purple
strain from South America, is parent to some
of our favorite modern varieties.

In the Victorian language of flowers,
fuchsia means good taste.

———— ❧ ————

In the Chilean mountains, at an altitude of
four to five thousand feet, there grew a
beautiful, small plant called fuchsia. A British
sailor found this plant, so the story goes, and
brought it home to his wife in England. The
plant produced beautiful flowers never
before seen in Europe and created quite a
sensation in England. James Lee, an eminent
nurseryman, finally persuaded the sailor's
wife to sell him the plant for quite a tidy
sum.

COMMON NAME:  **gentian**
GENUS:  *Gentiana*
SPECIES, HYBRIDS, CULTIVARS:
*G. acaulis*—evergreen leaves; blue flowers
in late spring. *G. septemfida*—large, deep
blue flowers in mid summer. *G. andrewsii*
—bottle gentian; easy to grow in woodlands.
FAMILY:  Gentianaceae
BLOOMS:  summer
TYPE:  perennial
DESCRIPTION:  Gentian blue is a
favorite descriptive phrase, and the color of
the blossoms certainly deserves the attention
it has received. It is an indescribably
beautiful shade. Many native gentian species
are suitable for bringing into the garden. The
plants are low growing, reaching a height of
6 to 12 inches. Gentians are excellent to
include within a rock garden or on shaded
slopes.
CULTIVATION:  Most gentians are
grown from seed, but plants can be divided
in spring. *G. septemfida* can be propagated
by taking cuttings in spring. All species like
rich, moist soil and sun or partial shade.

Anyone wanting to grow gentian should be
aware of its place in the language of flowers.
Gentian is a symbol of ingratitude because it
so often died in cultivation.

In spite of this, gentian has been grown
and used for its medincial properties for
many centuries. Papyrus records show that
Egyptians used this plant in 1200 B.C.
Ancient Greeks and Romans wrote of
gentian, praising its value as medicine.

The genus was named for Gentius, King
of Illyria (180–167 B.C.). He was well known
for using gentians for medicines. A
Hungarian folk legend tells of King Ladislas,
whose people were stricken by the plague. In
desperation, this good king shot an arrow
into the air, begging the Lord to let it land on
a plant that would help his people. The
arrow landed on gentian, and the legend tells
us that the plant wrought miraculous cures
among these people.

Taken as an antiseptic, gentian was
useful in killing intestinal worms. It was also
used to control fever, as an antidote for
poison, to purify blood, to stimulate the
appetite, to calm digestion, to stop vomiting,
and to improve the liver. It is still used
externally for bee and wasp sting.

During the Middle Ages, gentian was
called felwort, *fel* meaning "gall," for the
plant was used to treat gallstones.

During the seventeenth century, the
roots were added to ale and beer to improve
flavor. Gentian wine became a popular
aperitif, and Germany and Austria were
known for their powerful gentian brandy,
which was thought to "comfort the heart."

*G. lutea* was probably one of the first
gentians cultivated in England and was
originally grown for its medicinal value. The
bitter-tasting roots caused this plant to be
called bitterwort or bitter plant. Later, the
plant was appreciated for its beauty and was
one of the first flowers chosen for the
eighteenth-century Blenheim Palace Gardens.

COMMON NAME: **geranium**
GENUS: *Pelargonium*
SPECIES, HYBRIDS, CULTIVARS:
*P. domesticum*—Martha Washington.
*P. hortorum*—common geraniums.
*P. peltatum*—trailing geranium.
FAMILY: Geraniaceae
BLOOMS: summer
TYPE: perennial (tender)
DESCRIPTION: One of our favorite pot plants, *Pelargonium* (popularly but erroneously called geranium) is characterized by bright green, lobed leaves and vividly colored blossoms. Colors include white, lavender, red, pink, or rose. Flowers can be single or double. Generally plants grow to a height of 18 to 24 inches.
CULTIVATION: Geraniums need full, direct sun and moderate watering. Frequent fertilizing will insure heavy bloom throughout the growing season. To propagate, take cuttings from the plants in fall and overwinter them indoors.

John Bartram, a famous American botanist, received seeds of geraniums in 1760, and these flowers soon became popular in the colonies. They became synonymous with home and hospitality and were a treasured part of the household goods carried by pioneers heading west.

Leaves of geraniums are pleasantly scented and have been hybridized to capitalize on this fragrance. Lemon, rose, and mint (among many others) are scents available in different geraniums. The leaves have often been used as spices and were used when roasting meats or to flavor jams and jellies.

Oil from geranium leaves was used by the French to make inexpensive perfumes, and by 1850 both Turkey and France were mass-producing geraniums for this purpose.

In the language of flowers, scarlet geranium is associated with stupidity and fear.

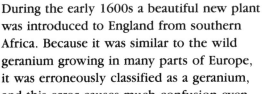

During the early 1600s a beautiful new plant was introduced to England from southern Africa. Because it was similar to the wild geranium growing in many parts of Europe, it was erroneously classified as a geranium, and this error causes much confusion even today. The popular garden plant that we call a geranium is not in the genus *Geranium* but in *Pelargonium*.

The name geranium comes from the Greek word *geranos*, meaning "crane," for the seed pods of the true geranium are long and pointed like a crane's bill.

Although the original strain was lost, many varieties of geraniums were brought from South Africa, and their popularity among Europeans was great, peaking late in the nineteenth century.

COMMON NAME: **geum**
GENUS: *Geum*
SPECIES, HYBRIDS, CULTIVARS:
*G. chiloense* (and hybrids). *G. heldreichii*
—double orange. *G.h.* 'Mrs. Bradshaw'
—bright red.
FAMILY: Rosaceae
BLOOMS: summer
TYPE: perennial
DESCRIPTION: Simple roselike flowers cover these airy plants during summer months. Colors include red, orange, and yellow. Plants reach a height of 18 to 24 inches. Basal leaves are generally evergreen in southern regions.
CULTIVATION: Geums do not like hot weather and demand constant moisture and soil that is high in organic matter. Many strains are not cold hardy. They do best in full sun in a moderate climate. It takes a few years for clumps to reach good size. To propagate, divide clumps after several years or sow seeds in spring.

Most of our most beautiful garden varieties of geum were developed from *G. chiloense*, a species found growing on the South American island of Chiloe.

The genus name is from the Greek word *geno*, meaning "giving perfume" or "to give an agreeable flavor," because roots of all members of this genus are so pleasantly scented. They are spicy, smelling like clove or cinnamon, and were stored with linens to keep them sweet smelling.

Geum was also used in cooking. A popular drink called Indian chocolate was made with the roots and leaves, water, wine, and sugar. The roots were also used to flavor gin.

The roots and leaves, according to John Gerard's *Herball*, were good for "internal injuries from falling from high places, stitches in sides and the bite from venemous insects." The English physician and scholar Culpeper said that it "warmeth a cold stomach and should be kept in everyone's house." The roots were also used to dissolve internal blood clots.

Geum was also known as avens, wood avens, or herb bennet, a shortened version of *herba benedicta*, meaning "blessed herb." Geum earned the name herb bennet because of its reputation for keeping away demons and evil spirits. The devil was thought to be powerless around the plant, so it was often brought indoors and the leaves and flowers were sometimes carved or painted on walls in churches.

Species with five golden yellow petals and leaves occurring in threes were thought to be symbolic of the Holy Trinity and the five wounds of Christ on the cross.

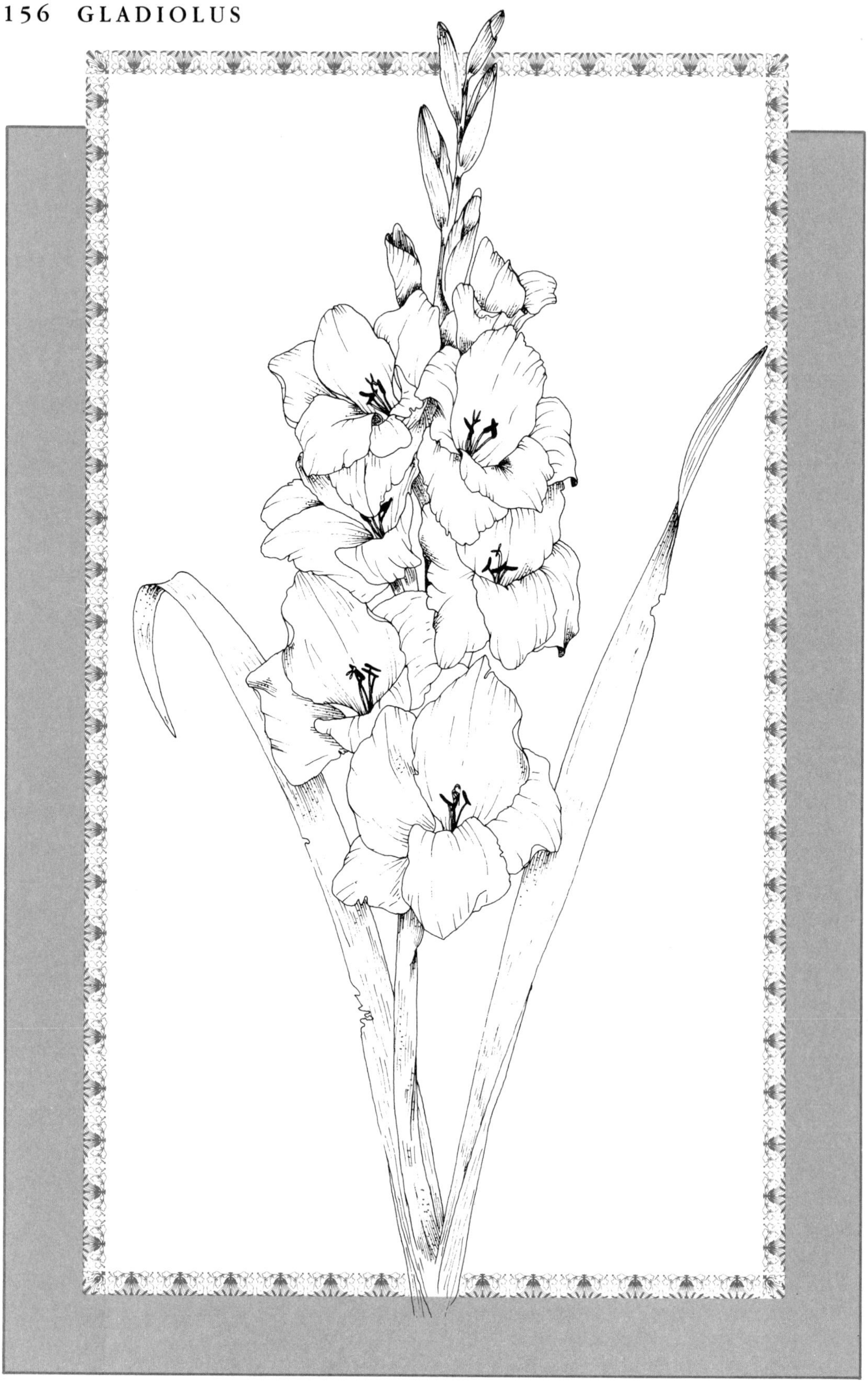

COMMON NAME: **gladiolus**
GENUS: *Gladiolus*
SPECIES: *G. gandavensis*
FAMILY: Iridaceae
BLOOMS: summer
TYPE: perennial
DESCRIPTION: Gladiolus puts forth tall spikes of very large, beautiful flowers. Blossoms come in almost every color, including white and a lovely green. The height of the "giants" and taller varieties is as much as 60 inches. Dwarf varieties grow as short as 24 inches.
CULTIVATION: Gladiolus grows from a corm planted three times its depth. Larger corms generally produce larger flowers. Plant corms 2 inches apart in an area that gets direct, bright sunlight. The plants are intolerant of any shade. Corms should be planted every week or two from mid-April through early August for successive blossoms. Flowers last only a single week.

Glads, as members of this genus are often called, are considered by many to be the second favorite of all cut flowers, losing out only to the rose in popularity.

Gladiolus is thought to be the "lilies of the field" that Jesus referred to in the Sermon on the Mount, for these grew quite wild and abundantly in the Holy Land and in the waste lands along the Mediterranean coast of Africa.

Because of the shape of the leaf, this plant has also been called sword lily, and in Rome it was considered the flower of the gladiators. The name gladiolus is from a Latin word meaning "sword."

Glads were first introduced to England in 1620 by John Tradescant, Sr., gardener to the English King Charles I.

Where gladioli grew wild, they were considered an important medicine, and this custom was passed on to England where they were grown primarily for their beauty. John Gerard in *Herball* wrote that a poultice made from the corms was good for drawing out splinters and thorns. The corms, dried and beaten to a powder, were added to breads or were mixed with goat's milk to treat colic.

Glads have been extensively hybridized and are available in many sizes and colors. Miniature hybrids were developed from the species *G. primulinus*, which was sent to Kew Gardens by Sir F. Fox, the engineer who built the bridge over the Zambesi River at Victoria Falls. This species grew within reach of the spray from the Falls and was known locally as maid in the mist.

This is the flower for August, according to the English floral calendar.

COMMON NAME: hibiscus

GENUS: *Hibiscus*

SPECIES, HYBRIDS, CULTIVARS:
*H. syriacus* (rose of Sharon)—deciduous.
*H. huegelii*—evergreen.

FAMILY: Malvaceae

BLOOMS: summer

TYPE: perennial

DESCRIPTION: A beautiful, colorful shrub, hibiscus gets as tall as 10 feet. It may be deciduous or evergreen, depending on the variety. The individual blossoms are 3 inches or more across, and colors range from white to blue, yellow, red, pink, purple, and even striped.

CULTIVATION: Hibiscus needs full sun and well-drained soil. Nearly one-third of the old wood should be removed with a spring pruning. Hibiscus forms a beautiful summer blooming hedge. Feed it early in the spring with a general fertilizer. This plant may need protection in northern areas or may even be grown as an annual in very cold climates.

———— ❀ ————

Hibiscus is the state flower of Hawaii.

Although most species in this genus are shrubs or house plants, some are suitable for the garden border.

The name hibiscus is from an ancient Greek name for "mallow," for this plant was thought to resemble the mallow blossom. The large blossoms, which are open for only a short time during the day, suggested other common names. Flower of an hour and good night at noon were both used to refer to the plant.

Originally from Africa, hibiscus was brought to England in the late sixteenth century.

Superstition in the South Sea Islands held that if a young girl placed a red hibiscus blossom behind her left ear, it signified "I desire a lover"; behind her right ear, it meant "I have a lover." Behind both ears, the message was "I have a lover but desire another."

Hibiscus blossoms are good for dyeing cloth and make wonderful tea. Fibers from the stems are sometimes used to make cloth.

COMMON NAME: hollyhock
GENUS: *Althaea*
SPECIES: *A. rosea*
FAMILY: Malvaceae
BLOOMS: summer
TYPE: annual, biennial, perennial
DESCRIPTION: Tall spires of large, richly colored blossoms can be shades of yellow, red, purple, pink, or white. The plants can grow to a height of 72 to 96 inches and blossoms are nearly 5 inches across.
CULTIVATION: Because of their height, hollyhocks will need staking. They need rich, deep soil and full sun. Annual varieties should be started indoors in March or outdoors after danger of frost has passed.

Hollyhocks have been a garden gem for many centuries. They were grown in ancient China both as an ornamental plant and as food. Peasants ate the leaves, cooked like other spring greens, and the flower buds, which were considered quite a delicacy.

The Romans found great use for hollyhock, using it as a potherb (greens that were gathered for food) and as an insect repellent. Leaves and flowers were strewn on the floors to help repel lice, fleas, and other insect pests.

The juice, which is mucilaginous, was used in cough syrups and was sometimes given to children for its calming and soothing powers. A poultice made from the roots and leaves was used on insect bites. Tea made from the flowers was thought to soothe the digestive tract and to relieve sores in the mouth or an inflamed throat. It was also good for "spongy gums" and was used to prevent miscarriages. The Arabs used it to treat uterine and vaginal infections.

The genus name is from the Greek word *althaea*, meaning "that which heals." The name hollyhock is from Anglo-Saxon words, *halig*, meaning "holy," and *hoc*, which was the name given to all members of this family. Halighoc was soon shortened to holihock, and later to hollyhock. It was given the term "holy" because it grows profusely in the Holy Land.

The name hockleaf comes from the ancient use of the plant to cure swollen heels of horses.

Hollyhocks were often planted beside beehives, for the bees made wonderful honey from the blossoms.

Because it is in the same family as cotton, hollyhocks have been investigated as a source of fibers for cloth. Two hundred and eighty acres of hollyhocks were planted near Flin, England, for this purpose, but the venture was not economically successful. Hollyhock was, however, found to be very good for dyeing cloth.

Hollyhocks were brought to North America in 1631, where they gained great popularity. They are still popular, primarily for their beauty, but also for their delicate unusual flavor. The following recipe for hollyhock sandwiches was suggested by Denise Diamond in her book *Living With Flowers*:

10 large hollyhock blossoms
2 avocados, sliced thin
10 pieces mild cheese, sliced thin
2 cups alfalfa sprouts

Layer avocado and cheese over blossoms. Top with sprouts, and your favorite dressing. Enjoy.

Hollyhock seed pods, which look like little wheels of cheese, are also edible.

Because of the abundance of blossoms, in the Victorian language of flowers, hollyhock means fruitfulness.

COMMON NAME: honesty
GENUS: *Lunaria*
SPECIES, HYBRIDS, CULTIVARS:
*L. annua*—purple. *L.a.* 'Alba'—white.
FAMILY: Cruciferae
BLOOMS: summer
TYPE: biennial
DESCRIPTION: During its second year of growth, lunaria produces intriguing and beautiful, round, silver seed pods. The flowers are small and fragrant but somewhat insignificant. The leaves are rather coarse looking.
CULTIVATION: Seeds should be sown in midsummer to allow collection of the seed pods the following year. Plants should be grown in full sun and well-drained soil.

——— ❧ ———

Since the flowers of honesty are rather common and inconspicuous, it is the seed pods that give this plant its magical appeal. These unusual-looking seed pods also gave the plant many different common names, including silver penny, silver shilling, moneywort, money plant, money in the pocket, pennyflower, money seed, white satin, satin seed, and satin pod. The sharp point at the end of the flower was used to prick out notes on thin paper before music was printed. Because of this, the plant was called prick-song. The name honesty was given the plant because one can see the seeds right through the transparent disc that holds them.

The genus name, *Lunaria*, was given to this plant because the round, silvery pods looked like a full moon, and lunaria is from the Latin word for moon.

Honesty was listed in an English herbal as a plant used to cast spells. Witches were said to use this plant to pull shoes off a horse, thus giving it the name unshoe-the-horse. Witches also were said to smear their broomsticks with lunaria, for it was supposed to make them fly better.

During the Dark Ages witches used honesty in their magical brews, because they believed that the plant held powers to open door locks, break chains, and banish monsters and demons.

Medicinal uses of the plant were limited, though a seventeenth-century Swiss physician mixed the leaves with oil and used it to dress wounds.

The roots, which have the biting taste characteristic of the Cruciferae (mustard) family, were sometimes eaten in salads.

According to the language of flowers, this plant was a symbol of honesty and fascination.

Honesty seed stalks are used extensively in dried flower arrangements. To dry them, gather the stalks as soon as the seeds start to turn brown. Rub off the outer part of the pod to expose the disk.

COMMON NAME: hosta
GENUS: *Hosta*
SPECIES, HYBRIDS, CULTIVARS:
*H. fortunei*—blue green leaves; violet
blossoms. *H. lancifolia*—narrow leaves;
blooms late. *H. plantaginea*—white
flowers; good ground cover. *H.
undulata*—bright green leaves with wavy
edges.
*H. ventricosa*—good for foliage and
flowers.
FAMILY: Liliaceae
BLOOMS: summer
TYPE: perennial
DESCRIPTION: Hostas are generally
grown for their beautifully variegated leaves,
although the gently colored flower spikes of
many species are an added attraction. Most
hosta flower stems grow to be 24 to 36
inches tall.
CULTIVATION: Variegated leaves will
perform best in partial shade; solid colors
will attain greatest depth in full sun. In
southern regions, the protection of shade is
necessary for all varieties. The plants look
wonderful in masses. Soil should be
moderately rich and should contain high
amounts of organic matter, and the plants
should be watered generously during the
growing season. Set out new plants or divide
old clumps in early spring.

Part of this neglect might be due to the fact
that it is so easy to grow many gardeners felt
that it was not worth their attention.

Much confusion about the names still
exists. This plant was first called funkia, and
then the name was changed to hosta.
Because the flowers last only a single day,
they were sometimes called day lilies, thus
confusing them with *Hemerocallis* species.

Popularity of these plants is spreading,
however, and many new strains have been
recently developed. In 1968 the Chelsea
Flower Show had an entire stand competely
filled with different varieties of hostas.

---

This favorite of the shade garden was named
for Nicholas Host (1761–1834), doctor to the
emperor of Austria. It is also commonly
called plantain lily because the leaves of
hostas and plantains are similarly shaped.

Although it has been known to
European gardeners for quite some time (the
first species was described in England in
1780), it was virtually ignored until recently.

COMMON NAME: impatiens

GENUS: *Impatiens*

SPECIES, HYBRIDS, CULTIVARS:
*I. wallerana* 'Elfin' series—6 to 12 inches;
'Imp' series—12 to 24 inches.

FAMILY: Balsaminaceae

BLOOMS: summer

TYPE: annual

DESCRIPTION: Impatiens is a popular
summer bedding plant used by the thousand
by homeowners across the country. The
leaves are small, roundish, and slightly lobed.
Colors range from white to pink, salmon,
orange, and red, and flower forms can be
single or double.

CULTIVATION: Impatiens is quite an
adaptable garden plant. It blooms well in
shade, semishade, or even full sun if given
sufficient moisture. It wilts easily if not
supplied with enough water, but revives
quickly when watered. These low-growing,
extremely free-flowering plants are suitable
for flower beds, hanging baskets, pots, or
large containers.

available. Because of their long growing
season and their profusion of blooms, they
are a staple of the summer garden.

Dr. Edward Bach, an early
twentieth-century English physician, often
prescribed a concoction made from the oil
of pink impatiens mixed with brandy. This,
he believed, was particularly useful for those
who were overanxious or irritable.

One of the most abundant native
impatiens is *I. capensis*, commonly known
as jewelweed. The sap of this plant contains
chemicals that act as a fungicide and are
particularly effective against the rash caused
by poison ivy. It was used by several North
American Indian Tribes to treat various skin
disorders.

Over 600 species make up this genus. Most
of these are native to Asia and Africa. Only
six species are native to North America and
Central America.

The name impatiens comes from a Latin
word meaning "impatient" and refers to the
action of the seed pods. As they mature, the
pods coil tightly and when disturbed, shoot
their seeds forth in a most impatient manner.
Because of this characteristic they are also
sometimes called snapweed and
touch-me-not.

The impatiens that we grow most often
in our gardens has been hybridized from an
East African species, *I. wallerana*. In the
past it was known as sultana or busy lizzie.
Many varieties of these plants are now

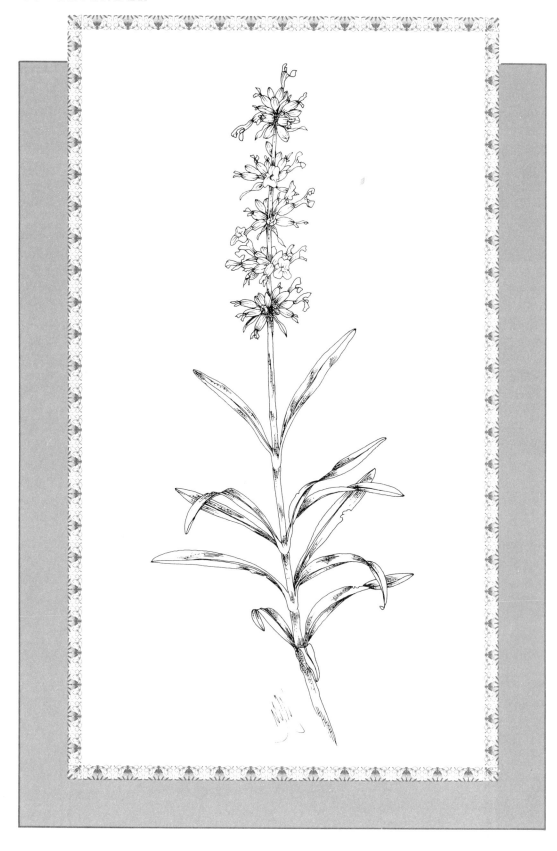

COMMON NAME: lavender
GENUS: *Lavandula*
SPECIES, HYBRIDS, CULTIVARS: *L. angustifolia* 'Munstead'—12 inches tall. *L.a.* 'Hidcote'—deep purple blue flowers; height and spread 18 inches. *L.a. 'Jean Davis'*—very hardy; white blossoms tinged with pink.
FAMILY: Labiatae
BLOOMS: summer
TYPE: perennial
DESCRIPTION: The gray green leaves of this plant are almost as attractive as the dense spikes of purple blue flowers. It has a compact, dense growth and is technically considered a subshrub.
CULTIVATION: Lavender needs well-drained soil and full sun. It does particularly well in raised beds. Beautiful when massed or perhaps used as a low flowering shrub, lavender should be cut back in fall and mulched heavily in winter. Seeds can be sown in spring, or cuttings can be taken during summer months.

The flowers and young shoots were made into a solution used as a mouthwash and gargle. Used regularly, it was thought to be good for the gums.

According to ancient superstition, if you carry a piece of lavender with you, you will be able to see ghosts. And if this plant thrives in the garden, the young ladies of the house will never marry, for lavender supposedly will grow only in an old maid's garden.

The plant was thought to have received its sweet scent when Mary washed the Christ Child's clothes and was looking for a place to hang them to dry. She chose the lavender bush, and when the sun and wind had dried the clothes and she went to get them, they smelled sweet and clean. The plant still smells this way today.

According to the Victorian language of flowers, lavender is a symbol of distrust.

---

Although lavender is appreciated for its beautiful flowers, it is the sweet scent that makes this plant unforgettable. The name lavender comes from the Latin word *lavare*, "to wash." This stemmed from the Roman custom of using the leaves and flowers of lavender to scent the bath water, a custom that is still practiced today. Lavender in the bath is thought to be soothing to sore muscles.

William Turner's *Herball*, written in 1551, suggests that "flowers of lavender quilted in a cap, comfort the brain very well." The flowers were also used externally to relieve the pain from headaches and to calm anger.

COMMON NAME: **lupines**
GENUS: *Lupinus*
SPECIES, HYBRIDS, CULTIVARS:
*L. polyphyllus* 'Russell' strain
FAMILY: Leguminosae
BLOOMS: summer
TYPE: perennial
DESCRIPTION: Tall, stately spires of pealike flowers appear in shades of pink, purple, red, blue, white, yellow, and bicolors. The leaves have many leaflets that look like fingers of a hand. They are dark green, handsome, and rarely get taller than 18 inches. The flower spikes often get to be 36 to 60 inches tall.
CULTIVATION: Lupines need full sun, lots of moisture, and rich soil. They suffer during hot summer weather and are unsuitable for growing in many areas. They do not like alkaline soil, so do not plant them in areas where lime has been applied. The areas where they grow best include parts of the West Coast, the Pacific Northwest, New England, and other northern states. Plants should be set out in early spring. Established plants should be divided in spring.

Because lupines originally grew in such poor soil, ancient people believed that lupines destroyed the nutrients in the soil, or "wolfed" them down. For this reason, they named the plant after lupus, the wolf. Another common name is wolf's bean. The shape of the blossom suggested other names such as old maid's bonnet or blue bonnet.

Acutally, like other members of the Leguminosae family, lupines add nitrogen to the soil. Early Romans and Egyptians used the plant for fertilizing the soil and as food for themselves and their cattle. The seeds have been found to contain a protein content 35 to 40 percent higher than that of peas or beans and have a very low oil content. People in many Mediterranean countries have eaten the seeds for centuries, soaking them to remove the bitterness and then boiling them to a mush.

The seeds were recommended by Pliny, a Roman statesman, as an aid to digestion. They have also been used extensively for skin care, especially for cleaning facial skin and removing spots.

During Roman times the flat seeds were used in the theater as stage money.

Lupines were first cultivated in English gardens in 1827 when David Douglas with the Horticultural Society of London grew a North American species, *L. ornatus*.

The flowers are useful for dyeing cloth. The scent from the blossoms is like that of honey.

COMMON NAME:  lychnis
GENUS:  *Lychnis*
SPECIES, HYBRIDS, CULTIVARS:
*L. chalcedonica* (Maltese cross)—30 inches;
bright scarlet flowers. *L. arkwrightii*
(hybrid of *L. chalcedonica* and
*L. haegeana*)—orange red; 18 inches.
FAMILY:  Caryophyllaceae
BLOOMS:  summer
TYPE:  perennial
DESCRIPTION:  Bright red flowers
sometimes make lychnis difficult to blend
with other flowers. Used as a focal point in
the garden, however, it can be very beautiful.
The flowers are borne in dense clusters. The
leaves are deep bronze purple. The stems are
stiff, making them good for cutting.
CULTIVATION:  Lychnis needs
well-drained, but average, soil and can
withstand moderately dry conditions. It will
bloom best in full sun but does not like
excessive heat and might do better with a bit
of shade in southern climates. The plants
grow quickly and will need dividing every
three to four years. Seeds of *L. chalcedonica*
can be sown into the flower bed in July and
will produce flowers the following spring.

The name catchfly was given because
the plant has a sticky stem that traps insects.

Lychnis was, according to legend,
brought back to France by Louis IX from the
Holy Land and probably came to England
during the Crusades. The English, French,
Spanish, Italians, and Germans referred to it
as Jerusalem cross, and the Portuguese called
it Maltese cross. Native to Russia, it was
sometimes known as flower of
Constantinople.

Because lychnis resembled a flower
grown near Bristol, it was sometimes called
flower of Bristow. Other English names
included nonesuch, knight's cross, scarlet
lightning, Bridget in her bravery, and robin
goodfellow.

Lychnis is thought to have sprung from
the bath water of Venus.

Lychnis goes by many names. The genus was
named for the Latin word for lamp, because
the petals of some species are flame colored.
It was also sometimes called lamp flower
because the soft, downy leaves were used to
make candlewicks.

It is also often called campion, perhaps
from the Latin word *campi*, meaning "field,"
for it was often found growing in open
fields. Or the name may have originated
when some species were used to make
garlands for victors, or champions, of public
games and tournaments; campion is similar
to the word champion.

COMMON NAME: **marigold**
GENUS: *Tagetes*
SPECIES, HYBRIDS, CULTIVARS:
*T. erecta*—African marigold; large, double flowers in white, cream, yellow, orange; tall.
*T. patula*—French marigold is shorter; double flowers in yellow and orange tones.
*T. tenuifolia*—signet marigold produces masses of single flowers and grows 8 inches tall.
FAMILY: Compositae
BLOOMS: summer
TYPE: annual
DESCRIPTION: Great variation exists among marigolds. They range in height from 6 to 36 inches, come in all shades of yellows, oranges, dark reds, and white, and have flowers that are single or double. Flower size can be as small as 3/4 inch across or as large as 5 inches across.
CULTIVATION: Marigolds are hardy, easy to grow, and adaptable to a wide range of conditions. However, they need full sun and prefer soil rich in organic matter. They come easily from seeds, which should be sown outdoors in flower beds after the last frost, or they can be started indoors six weeks before setting out.

In 1985 over 300 million marigold plants were grown in the United States, a fact that would probably amaze the Portugese explorers who first found these small yellow flowers growing in the wilds of Brazil in the early sixteenth century.

The marigold was considered sacred to the Aztec Indians who used it extensively to decorate shrines and temples. They considered it a living symbol of the Spanish massacre of their people, the red on the yellow blossoms representing the blood of Indians spilled on gold that the Spaniards had seized. It was sometimes known as *flor de muerto*, the "flower of death." Because of this history, the language of marigold is pain and grief.

The Portuguese took seeds of marigold to India where they adapted quite well and became so popular that they were soon considered the sacred herb of the Hindus. Marigolds were also sent to northern Africa, where one species grew so profusely it was soon called the African marigold. A dwarf variety became quite popular in Parisian gardens, and this strain became known as the French marigold.

The common name marigold comes from Mary's gold and honors the Virgin Mary. Because of this association, the flowers were considered powerful tokens of good luck and were thought to be protection against evil and witchcraft.

The genus name, *Tagetes*, is from the Etruscan god Tages, who first taught men the art of divining.

The aromatic leaves were used to heal wounds and rid of warts, and the blossoms make a good yellow dye. The plant has also proven to be effective in controlling pests in the vegetable garden. Chemicals within the root, when released into the soil, kill nematodes.

In Mexico marigolds are grown by the acre because the dried heads are sold to manufacturers of chicken feed. Marigold blossoms in the feed add color to egg yolks and give the flesh of the fryers a rich color.

Early naturalists called the plant "wife of the sun," for some species open in the morning and close at night.

The dried blossoms are edible and are even quite tasty added to scrambled eggs or other egg or cheese dishes.

**COMMON NAME:** morning glory
**GENUS:** *Ipomoea*
**SPECIES, HYBRIDS, CULTIVARS:**
*I. purpurea* 'Pearly Gates'—white.
*I.p.* 'Heavenly Blue'—blue. *I.p.* 'Early Call Rose'—rose-colored flowers stay open late in the day.
**FAMILY:** Convolvulaceae
**BLOOMS:** summer
**TYPE:** annual
**DESCRIPTION:** The trumpet-shaped flower of morning glories now comes in a delightful array of colors from the original blue form to white, red, rose-lavender, and white with blue stripes. The flowers are usually single, but double varieties are also sometimes available. The blossoms occur on slender vines that can climb over 10 feet if given sufficient support. Blossoms open first thing in the morning but close up as the sun gets hot.
**CULTIVATION:** Morning glory comes very easily from seeds, but they need pretreating before sowing. Wrap the seeds in a damp paper towel and keep them warm and moist for forty-eight hours. Plant them outdoors in small hills in late spring, and thin to 12 to 18 inches apart. These plants will grow in relatively poor soil. Once the plants are established, they are drought tolerant.

The family name, Convolvulaceae, is from the Latin word *convolvere*, meaning "to entwine," and is descriptive of how most plants in this family grow. The genus name, *Ipomoea*, is from two Greek words, meaning "similar to bindweed," for morning glory shares a great number of characteristics with the common bindweed.

Members of this family have collected quite a few common names including devil's guts and old man's nightcap, referring to the tendrils on the stem ends.

All parts of the plant, except the roots, are considered poisonous. Chemicals found within the plant are hallucinogenic and are potentially dangerous. The seeds, which were sometimes made into necklaces or bracelets, can cause a severe rash. Tinctures from the blossoms were used to treat headaches, rheumatism, and sore eyes.

Witches also found a use for the plant. The stems, wrapped around a person nine times, were thought to be effective in casting a wicked spell. This magic was particularly strong if the plant was used three days before a full moon.

The roots of morning glory, dried and pounded into a powder, have been used extensively as a laxative.

Morning glory is the flower for September, according to the English floral calendar. In the Victorian language of flowers, it is a symbol of affectation.

Morning glory has been called life of man throughout rural England. This is based on the blooming pattern of the plant: budding in the morning, opening fully by noon and wilting by evening.

Morning glories were first found growing in Mexico and were sent from there to Spanish monasteries. The monks frequently used morning glory designs on the borders of their manuscripts.

COMMON NAME:  nasturtium
GENUS:  *Tropaeolum*
SPECIES:  *T. major; T. minor*
FAMILY:  Tropaeolaceae
BLOOMS:  summer
TYPE:  annual
DESCRIPTION:  Very colorful, five-petaled blossoms grow on short or trailing plants. The leaves are round and attractive. Blossom colors include red, pink, and yellow and hues in between.
CULTIVATION:  Nasturtiums are very adaptable and can grow in poor soils and under drought conditions. They need well-drained soil and plenty of hot sunshine.

The genus name, *Tropaeolum*, is from a Greek word meaning "to twine" and is descriptive of the growth habit of many species within this genus. Another possible explanation of the origin of this name is the Greek word for trophy, *tropaion*, for to some people the flowers looked like a Roman helmet or round shield.

*T. minor*, first found growing in Mexico and Peru, has been in cultivation since the middle of the sixteenth century. Nicolas Monardes, a physician from Seville who wrote the first herbal about New World plants (*Joyfull Newes Out of the Newe Founde Worlde*), introduced nasturtiums to England in 1574. He called them Flowers of Blood, a translation of their Spanish name. Because of the tartness of the leaves, the English called this new plant Indian cress. Its larger cousin, *T. major*, was not introduced to the garden until over a hundred years later. Other common names included canary flower, yellow larkspur, and lark's heel.

The name *nasturtium* is from Latin words meaning "nose twister."

Nasturtiums have been used extensively for their taste and medicinal value. Sailors took barrels of pickled seeds on long voyages and ate them to combat scurvy. The pickled seeds were eaten like capers. Eating nasturtium blossoms was said to soften the muscles, or keep them from getting stiff. Oil from the seeds was rubbed on the body after exercising for this same purpose.

Eating nasturtiums is still popular today. The leaves can be eaten raw in salads, and the blossoms serve as colorful holders for dips or sandwich fillers.

To make Stuffed Naturtiums, mix together 8 ounces of cream cheese, one small can of drained crushed pineapple, and ¹/₄ cup of chopped pecans (or walnuts). Form this mixture into small balls and carefully stuff each ball into a large, firm nasturtium blossom.

COMMON NAME: **petunia**
GENUS: *Petunia*
SPECIES, HYBRIDS, CULTIVARS:
*P. grandiflora*—large flowers.
*P. multiflora*—prolific bloomer.
FAMILY: Solanaceae
BLOOMS: summer
TYPE: annual
DESCRIPTION: Petunia flowers come in quite an array of candy-store colors including red, pink, dark blue, light blue, purple, and yellow. The flowers are single or double and can be as wide as 7 inches across. The leaves are light green and somewhat sticky. Many varieties are trailing and creeping and good to use in hanging baskets.
CULTIVATION: Heat and drought tolerant, petunias are a favorite summer bedding plant all over the country. Start seeds indoors eight to ten weeks before you set out the plants, after danger of frost has passed. Place them in full sun in average soil. The blooming period can be extended by removing the spent blossoms.

Spanish explorers first found petunias growing near the coast of Argentina in the early sixteenth century. That first species was a low-growing, trailing plant with a fragrant white flower and was not of particular beauty. The Indians called it *petun*, or "worthless tobacco," and the plant was not thought to be of sufficient value to be sent back to Spain.

Three hundred years later, after the Napoleonic Wars had put Napoleon's brother Joseph Bonaparte on the Spanish throne, French explorers were sent to Argentina. They sent plant specimens back to Europe to be identified, and botanists there confirmed the Indian name for petunia and placed it in the tobacco family. The plant was then made available to European gardeners but was essentially ignored.

In 1831 another species of petunia was found in Argentina and sent to Europe, but again it gained no popularity there. It was not until plant breeders in the United States began extensive hybridization work on petunias and produced a miraculous variety of plant forms and colors that petunias began to receive favorable attention. Now petunias are enormously popular. They are quite adaptable and will grow in each one of the fifty states. This plant's ability to withstand drought conditions has earned the love and admiration of gardeners everywhere.

COMMON NAME: **phlox**
GENUS: *Phlox*
SPECIES, HYBRIDS, CULTIVARS:
*P. paniculata*—includes varieties in many colors ranging from white to pink, purple, and red. *P.p.* 'White Admiral'—white. *P.p.* 'Bright Eyes'—light pink with dark pink centers. *P.p.* 'Vintage Wine'—claret red; blooms late in summer. *P. carolina*—only in white and pink; no problem with reversion *P.c.* 'Miss Lindgard'—mildew resistant; blooms June and July.
*P. divaricata*—blue phlox; blooms April and May in shady area; grows only 18 to 24 inches tall. Each of these are perennials.
*P. drummondii*—annual phlox; red or pink.
FAMILY: Polemoniaceae
BLOOMS: summer
TYPE: annual and perennial
DESCRIPTION: Beautiful and sweet smelling, phloxes provide an important part of the summer garden. Colors include white, red, pink, salmon, lavender blue, orange, and deep purple. The flower heads are attractive mounds of five-petaled florets. The plants begin to bloom around the first of July and continue to do so for many weeks.
CULTIVATION: The greatest problem in growing phloxes is the prevalence of mildew on the plants. Be extremely careful to avoid getting moisture on the leaves, and don't grow phlox plants near brick or stone walls that retain moisture. Many strains have been developed that are mildew resistant, and these are highly recommended. Phloxes do like moist roots, however. Water with a soaker hose instead of a general lawn sprinkler to keep the roots moist without getting the leaves and flowers wet.

Phlox blossoms were used extensively in Victorian England for sending messages through tussie-mussies and bouquets. Not only is their scent delightful, but their message is welcome, for phloxes mean a proposal of love and a wish for sweet dreams.

The word phlox is from a Greek word meaning "flame" and was given to this plant because many of the blossoms were red.

Phloxes have been among the most popular of all garden plants brought to Europe from North America. It was not cultivated in American gardens until it was reintroduced here from European horticulturists.

The leaves of phlox were sometimes crushed and added to water to cure such ailments as skin disorders, abdominal pain, and problems with eyes. The leaves were also used as a gentle laxative.

Phloxes are particularly cherished for their sweet scent. White and pale varieties are additionally appreciated for their luminosity and scent in the garden in early evening.

COMMON NAME: pincushion flower
GENUS: *Scabiosa*
SPECIES, HYBRIDS, CULTIVARS:
*S. atropurpurea*—annual; 24 to 48 inches
tall. *S. fama*—perennial; blue flowers.
*S. caucasica*—blue flowers; 30 inches tall.
FAMILY: Dipsacaceae
BLOOMS: summer
TYPE: annual or perennial
DESCRIPTION: Pincushion flower is
rather exotic looking, grows to a height of 18
to 48 inches and has blossoms 3 inches
across. The flowers have an intricate form,
with many ray flowers and a dome shape.
Colors include white, blue, maroon, and red.
CULTIVATION: Annual pincushion
flower comes easily from seed. Start the
seeds indoors, four to six weeks before you
set them out in a sunny spot in the garden.
The plants need good moisture during
summer months but very good drainage in
winter. They do not perform well in extreme
heat but are quite hardy otherwise. Grow
them in average soil.

Known as the most beautiful member of the
Teasel (Dipsacaceae) family, pincushion
flower has also been called sweet scabious
and mournful widow, a name based on the
fact that the first species brought to England
were very dark. According to the language of
flowers, pincushion flower meant "I have
lost all," and it was often used in funeral
wreaths and given to widows in mourning.

The genus name is from this plant's
alleged powers to heal skin disorders and
wounds.

Many species from this genus make
good cut flowers and dyes.

The common name pincushion flower
comes from the dotlike pistils that protrude
above the flower head.

COMMON NAME:  pinks
GENUS:  *Dianthus*
SPECIES, HYBRIDS, CULTIVARS:
*D. plumarius* 'Spring Beauty'—mixture of double flowers; colors range from pink to rose, salmon, and white with interesting markings. *D.p.* 'Essex Witch'—dwarf variety; only 5 inches tall; rose-pink; easy to grow. *D.p.* 'Aqua'—white, double flowers on stalks 10 to 12 inches tall.
*D. caryophyllaceae*—garden or florist carnation; 18 to 24 inches.
FAMILY:  Caryophyllaceae
BLOOMS:  summer
TYPE:  perennial
DESCRIPTION:  Members of the genus *Dianthus* include both the florist's carnation and the garden pinks. They are lovely, clove-scented flowers worthy of the attention they have received. Colors generally range in the pink and red tones, though there are white varieties, as well as a yellow species, *D. knapii*, native to Yugoslavia.
CULTIVATION:  Pinks grow best in very well drained, slightly alkaline soil. Optimum conditions include full sun but relatively cool weather. Keeping the faded flowers picked will lengthen the blooming period, and removing lateral buds promotes a larger and stronger center flower.

The sweet, spicy scent of pinks, combined with their lovely blossoms, has made these flowers favorites of kings and noblemen, as well as common folks, for many centuries. Pinks were thought to be the favorite flower of William the Conqueror, Edward III, Charles II, and George V.

All members of the genus *Dianthus* are called "pinks," including the species *D. caryophyllus*, the florist's carnation. The name pink is from the word *pinct*, which means "pinked" or "scalloped," referring to the jagged edges of the petals. To pink something is to cut a jagged edge, as you would do with pinking shears.

The earliest mention of carnations was in connection with the Crusaders, who were stricken with the plague near Tunis in the thirteenth century. They drank wine mixed with leaves of the pinks to help control the raging fevers. They took the flowers back to France, where they were called *tunica*.

Designs of carnations are found on tiles dating back to the fifteenth century, and it is thought that the Turks have been cultivating these flowers since the 1450s. Pinks became a symbol of the high point of civilization during Roman times. It was called the flower of flowers in ancient Greece, and the genus name means "divine flower" because of its fragrance and beauty. It was called *flos Jovis*, or "Jove's flower," in Rome.

Because the original flowers were flesh colored, they were called carnations, from the Latin word *carnatio*, meaning "flesh." A Christian legend tells us that when Mary saw Jesus carrying the cross, she began to cry, and where her tears fell, carnations began to grow. Perhaps because of this legend, the pink carnation became a symbol of a mother's love and in 1907 was chosen as the emblem for Mother's Day.

An Italian legend tells of a young woman, Margherita, who fell in love with a knight, Orlando. Orlando was called to war and carried with him a white carnation that Margherita had given him. When Orlando was mortally wounded, his blood stained the center of the flower. The flower was returned to the heartbroken Margherita, who planted the seeds. Every flower that came from these seeds was white with crimson centers. Margherita never married, and it became customary in her family to bring a vase of carnations to each baby girl born into the family.

During the Renaissance, pinks were associated with happiness and carefree days, and because of this, they were used to "combat melancholy and cheer the heart," according to an ancient herbal.

Carnations were at one time called gillyflowers, perhaps a corruption of the Italian word meaning "clove," for the spicy, clovelike scent.

John Gerard, in his sixteenth-century herbal, wrote that a conserve made from the flowers of pinks and sugar was good to "comfort the heart" and was useful in expelling poison and fevers. By the early seventeenth century, fifty varieties could be found growing in England.

For over 400 years, well into the eighteenth century, carnations were used to flavor beer, ale, and wine. Tavern keepers would sometimes grow this plant in their own gardens and called it sops-in-wine. In 1748 a recipe was published that recommended using carnations to dye the hair black.

In Korea, carnations were used to tell fortunes. A girl placed a cluster of three blossoms in her hair. If the top one died first, this signified that her last years would be difficult. If the middle one died first, the earlier years would be hard. If the bottom flower died first, superstition held that her entire life would be miserable.

In the Victorian language of flowers, yellow carnation means disdain and rejection, purple signifies antipathy and capriciousness, red means admiration, and white is pure and ardent love and a good-luck gift to a woman.

In addition to their beauty in the garden, carnations can also be used for their delicate flavor. The fresh petals can be chopped and added to sweet bread or muffin batter, or made into syrups or conserves.

Denise Diamond, in her book *Living with Flowers*, offers the following recipe for carnation syrup:

> 1 cup plain yogurt
> 6 to 10 pink carnations (petals only)
> $1/4$ cup apple juice
> $1/2$ cup ground almonds
> $1/2$ teaspoon cinnamon

Blend half the petals and yogurt in blender. Fold in remaining ingredients. Serve over pancakes or warm gingerbread.

COMMON NAME:  **portulaca**
GENUS:  *Portulaca*
SPECIES:  *P. grandiflora*
FAMILY:  Portulacaceae
BLOOMS:  summer
TYPE:  perennial (grown as an annual)
DESCRIPTION:  The creeping habit of portulaca makes it wonderful to use in rock gardens, hanging baskets or low flower beds. The plant rarely grows taller than 8 inches. The leaves are short and narrow but thick and fleshy. The blossoms look like single or double roses, measure 1 1/2 to 2 inches across, and come in nearly every shade of red and yellow. New strains have been developed that stay open all day, unlike some of the earlier varieties that closed by noon.
CULTIVATION:  Portulaca is heat and drought tolerant and thrives during a long, hot summer. Sow the seeds in full sun in the garden after the last spring frost and then thin the plants to 10 to 12 inches apart. Blooms should appear eight weeks after sowing. Do not water portulaca too frequently; the plant blooms more prolifically when kept on the dry side.

Because it is mucilaginous, this plant has many uses in cooking, such as to thicken soups and stews. The leaves and flowers could be eaten cooked, raw, or pickled. It has a very mild, pleasant taste.

Portulaca also reputedly held magical properties: placed on a child's bed, it would keep away evil spirits as the child slept.

A German legend tells of the origin of portulaca, or moss rose, as it is sometimes called: An angel walking through a forest became tired and sat underneath a rose tree to rest. When she awoke, the angel thanked the tree for its hospitality and offered to spread a carpet of moss underneath its branches to keep its roots cool. This moss we now call moss rose.

The name portulaca comes from the Latin *portula*, meaning "little gate," for the top of the seed capsule opens like a gate.

———— ❦ ————

Protulaca was first introduced from South America to European gardeners in the early 1700s. Although its beauty as a garden flower was much appreciated, it was also considered quite useful medicinally for such complaints as teeth set on edge or burning from gunpowder. Because portulaca has a very high iron and vitamin content, the leaves were also eaten as a vegetable and were good to cure scurvy. Placed on the neck, portulaca was thought to relieve muscle spasms or neck cricks. Putting it under the tongue was supposed to prevent thirst. However, eating portulaca was thought to stimulate the appetite.

COMMON NAME: red-hot poker
GENUS: *Kniphofia*
SPECIES: *K. uvaria*
FAMILY: Liliaceae
BLOOMS: summer
TYPE: perennial
DESCRIPTION: This unusual member of the lily family has a tall spike of orange and yellow flowers. The deepest shades of orange are found at the top of the flowering spike, and the color gets progressively lighter and turns to yellow toward the bottom. New strains of this plant have introduced other color variations. The plant reaches a height of 24 to 40 inches. The foliage is tall, coarse, and grasslike and lends interesting texture to the summer garden.
CULTIVATION: Red-hot poker needs full sun to light shade and a somewhat sheltered spot, for it cannot withstand heavy frosts. In very cold regions, provide some sort of protective mulch or cover. The plants will survive extreme heat and considerable drought but perform much better with regular watering.

Originally known as tritoma, red-hot poker is from the Cape of Good Hope in Africa and was brought to Europe in 1707. In England it was considered a greenhouse plant until it was planted in the flower borders at Kew in 1848.

The *Kniphofia* genus was renamed for Dr. Johann Hieronymous Kniphof, the author of a twelve-volume set of herbals. The illustrations for this set were made by putting ink directly on the specimen and stamping the image on the page.

The common name refers to the bright red color of the plant and the tall, spikelike configuration of the blossoms. Another common name is torch lily. The species name *uvaria* is Latin, meaning "clustered," and describes the blossoms.

COMMON NAME: rose
GENUS: *Rosa*
SPECIES, HYBRIDS, CULTIVARS:
Types of roses: Old-fashioned—includes the
older hybrids. Hybrid tea—large blooms.
Floribundas—smaller blossoms borne in
clusters. Modern shrub—large flowered.
Climbers and ramblers—vigorous climbing
habit. Miniature—tiny, with semi-double or
double flowers.
FAMILY: Rosaceae
BLOOMS: summer
TYPE: perennial
DESCRIPTION: It is difficult to find
any flower more beautiful than roses. The
grace and elegance of the flower forms and
richness of their colors make them true
beauties of the garden. New varieties
constantly come on the market to compete
with the popular old-fashioned roses that
have been known and loved for centuries.
CULTIVATION: Rose gardens should be
created in an open, airy spot in full sun with
rich, deep soil. Dig the area 1 foot deep and
allow it to settle before planting. Roses
require a good bit of care. They should be
watered regularly, fed periodically, and
checked frequently for pests or disease.
Pruning is necessary to cut out dead or weak
branches and to clip out lateral buds to
produce larger center flowers.

———— ❧ ————

Chloris, the Greek goddess of flowers,
crowned the rose queen of all flowers, a title
that the rose deserves today as much as it did
in the Golden Age of Greece. Not only is the
rose of unparalleled beauty, it has also
proved itself to be useful in a hundred
different ways. It has been prized for its
medicinal value, cherished for its sweet
scent, and appreciated for its delicate flavor.

The legend of the origin of the rose is
from the days of the Roman Empire. The
story is told of Rhodanthe, a woman of such
exquisite beauty that she had many, many
suitors. She showed little interest in any of
them and sought refuge in the Temple of
Diana. Her suitors were persistent, however,
and followed her there, breaking down the
gates to get close to her. Diana became
incensed at this and turned Rhodanthe into a
beautiful rose and the suitors into thorns.
From this legend, the rose has become a
symbol for love and beauty.

Romans used roses extravagantly, and
soon they became synonymous with woman,
wine, and the indulgent mood of that day.
Because of this, early Christians would not
allow roses in the church.

Medieval gardens always included many
roses. These were not grown so much for
their beauty as for food, for medicine, and to
supply materials to make rosaries (made from
compressed rose petals).

Roses were thought to cure a wide
vareity of ailments, including toothaches and
earaches; diseases of the stomach, lungs, and
intestines; overindulgence in wine;
headaches; hemorrhages, sleeplessness;
excessive perspiration; and hydrophobia.
According to the doctrine of signatures, red
roses were used to treat nosebleeds.

The rose is dedicated to Harpocrates,
god of silence. The term *sub rosa*, "under
the rose," comes from the Roman practice of
hanging a rose or swag of roses over a
conference table. The code of honor was
that no gossip passed at the table under the
roses could be repeated. Today sub rosa
means confidential or in secret.

Roses have been cultivated in Greece
and the Orient for over 3,000 years. It is
thought that all cultivated roses came from
the dog rose, *R. canina*. Fossils of this rose
species from 35 million years ago have been
found in Montana.

One of the first lavish displays of roses
was seen in England in the seventeenth
century when Catherine of Braganza (from

Portugal) married Charles II of England, and roses were brought from the Orient for the ceremony. This helped to open up the Orient to the British, and the British India Company soon opened botanical gardens in Singapore and Calcutta.

The rose adapted exceedingly well to the English climate and quickly gained great popularity there.

The English Wars of the Roses were fought between the House of York (symbolized by a white rose) and the House of Lancaster (whose symbol was a red rose).

During World War II the nutritional value of rose hips (from the dog rose) was discovered. Rose hips contains more vitamin C than almost any fruit or vegetable. Gathering rose hips became a national passion for a time, and the dog rose was a patriotic symbol.

To the Arabs, roses signified masculine beauty, and the white rose was often associated with Mohammed. The Arabs brought the art of distilling to Europe and rose essence soon became an important ingredient in perfumes, cooking, and medicines. Roses were used extensively as flavoring and were important in making candy.

Josephine Bonaparte, Napoleon's empress, was an ardent rose lover and had a collection of over 250 varieties.

Associations with the rose were not always happy. In Switzerland roses were often associated with death, and cemeteries were sometimes called rose gardens. Ancient Saxons believed that when a child died, one could see the image of death plucking a rose. The rose also symbolized rebirth and resurrection.

Cultivated roses arrived in North America in the early seventeenth century when Samuel de Champlain brought roses from France to plant in his garden in Quebec. The greatest rose collection in the New World in 1630 was held by Peter Stuyvesant in New Netherland. Although twenty-six species of roses are native to North America, over 90 percent of those grown in cultivation are non-native.

Americans have always loved the rose. It is the state flower of New York, and the American Beauty Rose is the floral emblem of Washington, D.C. In 1986 the rose was chosen as the national flower of the United States.

The Shakers grew roses extensively and used the petals to make rose water, which they sold. The Shaker Rose Rule was that no rose could be cut to use for decoration or personal enjoyment. All roses were cut without stems and were used only to make rose water.

Perhaps the most famous quotation about roses is from Shakespeare's *Romeo and Juliet*: "What's in a name? That which we call a rose by any other name would smell as sweet." Roses have never been known by any other name, and their scent today remains as hauntingly sweet as it was 3,000 years ago when roses were grown in the Orient.

COMMON NAME: **Saint John's wort**
GENUS: *Hypericum*
SPECIES: *H. calycinum,*
*H. hookerianum, H. patulum*
FAMILY: Hypericaceae
BLOOMS: summer
TYPE: perennial
DESCRIPTION: Saint John's wort is a low-growing, partly woody perennial that produces bright yellow flowers from early summer until frost. The flowers, which measure 1 1/2 to 2 inches across, occur in groups of five to seven. The plant reaches a height of 40 to 60 inches, though dwarf varieties that grow only 18 to 24 inches tall are available. Light green leaves have a silver lining.
CULTIVATION: A hardy plant, Saint John's wort thrives in poor soil and full sun or light shade. The top of the plant might be killed back in severe winter weather but this does not seem to affect its performance, since the blossoms appear on new spring growth.

Sun and light are images often associated with Saint John's wort. The genus was thought to have been named for the Greek Titan Hyperion, father of Helios, god of the sun. According to Teutonic mythology, this plant was dedicated to the sun god, Baldur. It was called the herb of destiny and was thought to be marked by the sun. Small, translucent, sunlike circles appear on the leaves and flowers. The species name *perforatum* refers to these circles. *H. perforatum* is a European species widely naturalized in North America.

The history of this plant includes many mystical happenings. As part of certain pagan rituals, it was burned on Midsummer's Eve to honor the sun and placate the good fairies. On the Isle of Wight it was believed that if you stepped on Saint John's wort after dark, a phantom horse would sweep you up and carry you on a wild ride, lasting until dawn. Saint John's wort was also called demon chaser.

Early Christians opposed heathen rituals and tried to put an end to many of these pagan celebrations. Because John the Baptist was born on Midsummer Day, they changed the name of this plant to Saint John's wort and said that Saint John had blessed it with many healing powers. The ancient Feast of Fires was changed to the Feast of Saint John, celebrated on June 24.

This plant was grown in monastery gardens during medieval times because of its value in healing wounds and treating inflammation of the lungs and throat. In Brazil this plant was used as an antidote for snakebites. In Russian it was considered protection against hydrophobia. An early twentieth-century herbal suggests that a concoction made from this plant was good for coughs and colds. According to the doctrine of signatures, the translucent holes in the leaves indicated that the plant would be useful in healing holes or cuts in the body.

Saint John's wort was brought to America by Rosicrucians, members of a mystical religious sect from Germany who arrived on American shores on Midsummer's Eve day.

The Pennsylvania Dutch called it "blessed herb" and considered it protection for newborn children, saying that a sprig over the doorway would banish the evil eye.

COMMON NAME: salvia
GENUS: *Salvia*
SPECIES, HYBRIDS, CULTIVARS:
*S. splendens*—popular bedding plant grown
as an annual. *S. superba* 'Blue Queen'
—perennial; short spikes of deep violet
flowers. *S. haematodes*—perennial; to 36
inches; sprays of lavender flowers.
FAMILY: Labiatae
BLOOMS: summer
TYPE: annual and perennial
DESCRIPTION: Both annual and
perennial salvias are characterized by
attractive spikes of flowers. The
bedding-plant salvia produces brilliant spikes
of red flowers above dark green leaves. The
annual salvia also can be found in white and
dark purple. Given sufficient moisture
through the growing season, these plants can
reach a height of 30 inches.
CULTIVATION: Both annual and
perennial forms of salvia need full sun and
well-drained soil. Set plants out after the last
spring frost, or sow seeds indoors six to
eight weeks before setting them out. In hot
areas these plants might do best with a bit of
afternoon shade.

The genus *Salvia* is a very large one and
includes several aromatic herbs used
extensively in cooking.

The red garden salvia was considered
too intensely colored for the tastes of most
English gardeners, so it was exported to the
United States, where it gained great
popularity. The blue salvia, *S. patens*, was
first found growing in Mexico and was taken
to England in 1838.

The name salvia is from the Latin word
for "safe" or "healthy," because salvia was
used as medicine for many years. The
common name sage is from the same origin.
It was dedicated to the Greek god Zeus and
the Roman god Jupiter. Sage was used for
problems of the liver, stomach, heart, and
blood, and was used to cure epilepsy, fever,
and the plague. Sage was said to have its
hidden dangers as well, for an ancient
superstition said that a woman who drank
salvia cooked in wine would never be able to
conceive.

The bright blossoms of the plant were
used as a dye and are good for attracting
hummingbirds.

COMMON NAME: **spiderwort**
GENUS: *Tradescantia*
SPECIES, HYBRIDS: *T. andersoniana*
(hybrid of *T. bracteata* and *T. virginiana*)
FAMILY: Commelinaceae
BLOOMS: summer
TYPE: perennial
DESCRIPTION: The three petals of the
spiderwort blossom are gently scalloped and
beautifully colored. Hybrids developed from
two native North American species have
resulted in flowers in shades of blue, pinks,
reds, and white. The foliage is long, narrow,
and grasslike. This plant has a very long
blooming period, generally lasting from early
summer until frost. Blossoms close by
midday, but new flowers appear early the
next morning.
CULTIVATION: Spiderworts need rich,
well-drained soil but perform equally well in
full sun or light shade. Water them regularly,
and top-dress the plants in the fall with
organic matter.

were responsible for bringing many new
plants to England from the colonies.

Spiderwort is extremely sensitive to
varying levels of pollution and will quickly
undergo mutations that change the color of
the stamens. Recently it has been discovered
that not only is spiderwort useful in
indicating pollution from pesticides,
herbicides, auto exhaust, and sulphur
dioxide, but it is also extremely sensitive to
low levels of radiation. According to Norman
Myers's book *A Wealth of Wild Species*,
spiderwort may measure radiation levels
better than a mechanical counter, such as a
dosimeter, for the machine is limited to
detecting external exposure, whereas the
plant indicates internal damage as well. The
stamens of spiderwort change color in only
ten to fifteen days after exposure. Now being
marketed commercially by a company in
California, spiderwort is being used to detect
harmful pollution levels as well as the
presence of cancer-causing radiation.

Although spiderwort in its species form is
considered something of an aggressive weed,
the flowers resulting from hybridization are
lovely and the growth habit quite suited to
the formal garden.

The name spiderwort has several
possible origins. The leaves of the plant are
long and narrow, reminding some of spider
legs. This plant was used at one time as a
cure for spider bites.

Enzyme action within the plant causes
the flowers, after they have been pollinated,
not to shrivel when they die, but to turn into
a runny blob. This characteristic has given it
names like Moses in the bulrushes and
widow's tears.

The genus was named for John
Tradescant and his son, who were royal
gardeners to King Charles I of England. They

COMMON NAME: **statice**

GENUS: *Limonium*

SPECIES, HYBRIDS, CULTIVARS:
*L. bonduellii* and *L. sinuatum* are annuals
with clusters of yellow, blue, purple, or rose
flowers. *L. latifolium*—perennial; 28 to 30
inches tall; lavender flowers. *L.
perezii*—perennial; 36 inches tall; purple
and white flowers.

FAMILY: Plumbaginaceae

BLOOMS: summer

TYPE: annual and perennial

DESCRIPTION: Annual statice is a
multi-branched plant producing delicate
sprays of flowers that rise to a height of 24
inches. Many flower colors are available. The
leaves are large and leathery. The evergreen
leaves of perennial statice are even larger,
sometimes getting 12 inches long. The
flowering stems grow 30 to 36 inches tall
and produce blue or purple flowers. Plants
often spread as much as 36 inches across.

CULTIVATION: Statice likes good sun,
regular watering, and rich soil. The richer
the soil, the bigger the flower heads. Annual
varieties are started easily from seed, because
the seeds are exceptionally clean and free of
chaff.

———— ❦ ————

The flowers make wonderful cut or dried
flowers. For dried flowers, the blossoms
should be picked in prime condition and
should be hung upside down. The stems are
somewhat weak and if they are dried
upright, they often cannot support the
weight of the flowers as they dry.

The genus name is from the plant's
similarity to another plant, *leimonion*, which
grows in salt marshes. *Limonium* is native to
dry grasslands from southeastern Europe to
southeastern Russia.

COMMON NAME:  strawflower
GENUS:  *Helichrysum*
SPECIES:  *H. bracteatum*
FAMILY:  Compositae
BLOOMS:  summer
TYPE:  annual
DESCRIPTION:  The blossoms are pomponlike, measure 2½ inches across, and come in white and bright shades of yellow, red, pink, and orange. Plants grow about 2 to 3 feet tall, though dwarf varieties are available that are a mere 12 to 18 inches in height.
CULTIVATION:  Choose a sunny, dry spot in the garden and sow seeds of strawflower in spring after the last frost.

Over 500 aromatic perennial species make up this genus native to Crete and Asia Minor.

The most outstanding thing about this plant is the way its flowers retain their color and shape for a very long time. Everlasting, another common name, refers to this characteristic. The species *H. bracteatum* is called immortelle. Although grown most often for use as a dried flower, strawflowers also make good fresh cut flowers.

The plant contains chemicals that were at one time used in treating respiratory diseases, liver and gallbladder problems, rheumatism, and allergies.

The genus name is from two Greek words, *helios*, meaning "sun," and *chrysos*, meaning "golden."

Several species were used to make funeral wreaths and were grown extensively in southern France for this reason.

COMMON NAME:  sunflower
GENUS:  *Helianthus*
SPECIES:  *H. annuus*—grown for seed and  flower
FAMILY:   Compositae
BLOOMS:   summer
TYPE:   annual
DESCRIPTION:   Characterized by its height and size of flower, the sunflower has earned a welcome place in the summer garden. Many varieties on the market now offer diversity in color (even a white sunflower!), size of flower, and plant height. Dwarf plants grow only 15 inches tall.
CULTIVATION:   Extremely heat and drought tolerant, most sunflowers can easily exist under conditions unsuitable for growing many other garden flowers. Although the shorter strains can be grown in poor soils, the taller varieties need moderately rich soil and regular watering. They will also need staking. Sow seeds outdoors where you want them to grow. Depending on the size plant you are growing, thin the seedlings to 24 to 48 inches apart.

These towering plants, beacons of light and warmth, have been loved and worshipped for many centuries. The Incan Indians of Peru considered this flower a symbol of the sun and worshipped it accordingly. Priestesses of the temple wore sunflower medallions made of gold.

American pioneer families found many uses for sunflowers. New growth was eaten like asparagus, and the seeds were eaten as a tasty snack, used in baking, and fed to birds during winter months. The leaves and stalks were used as fodder, and fibers from the stalks were used to make cloth. Oil from the seeds was used in cooking and for making soap, and the blossoms made a good yellow dye. Not only were the plants grown in the garden, they were also planted close to the house because of the superstition that sunflowers were protection against malaria.

Sunflowers are native to North America, and South America, and many Indian tribes used the plant for cooking, mixing paint, and dressing their hair.

The genus name, *Helianthus*, is from two Greek words, *helios*, meaning "sun," and *anthos*, meaning "flower."

According to the Victorian language of flowers, sunflower is a symbol of haughtiness.

COMMON NAME: **verbena**

GENUS: *Verbena*

SPECIES, HYBRID, CULTIVARS:
*V. bipinnatifida*—light purple perennial; 3 inches tall. *V. rigida*—purplish blue perennial; 1 foot tall. *V. rigida* 'Flame'—red flowers from June through frost. *V. canadensis*—rose pink flowers from June through frost. *V. venosa*—purplish blue flowers; to 1 foot. *V. hybrida*—'Amethyst'—lavender blue; annual. *V.h.* 'Blaze'—scarlet; annual. *V.h.* 'Sangria'—wine colored; heat tolerant; annual; spreads 1 to 1½ feet.

FAMILY: Verbenaceae

BLOOMS: summer

TYPE: annual and perennial

DESCRIPTION: Low-growing verbena blooms profusely and adds great color to the summer perennial bed. Different species vary in height from 3 to 12 inches and in spread from 12 to 24 inches. Flowers are small and borne on short stalks; the foliage is bright green and continuously attractive. Verbenas come in white and bright shades of red, pink, blue, and purple.

CULTIVATION: Full sun and well-drained soil are necessary conditions for growing verbena, though it thrives in soil of average fertility. Seeds sown in spring will usually produce plants that bloom at the end of the first year. Many verbenas are treated as annuals. Seeds of these should be planted in sandy, well-drained soil during the middle of May. Pinching back the plants will keep them producing blooms and prevent them from getting lanky. Both perennial and annual types are quite drought tolerant.

The verbena found so often in our gardens today looks quite different from the native strains. The lemon verbena was found in the Andes Mountains of South America by Spanish conquistadors. The fragrance of this plant was said to be so powerfully sweet that the plant could be found by its scent alone. Unfortunately, as verbena has been hybridized to produce larger and more beautiful flowers, the power of its fragrance has diminished considerably.

Our garden verbena is closely realted to *V. officinalis*, a species native to this country but also grown in many European countries.

Both the early Greeks and Romans are thought to have used different species of verbena in many of their religious ceremonies. An infusion made from the blossoms was often sprinkled on the altar of Jupiter, the supreme god in Roman mythology. The entire plant was considered sacred to Mars, god of war, and was thought to have the power to drive away the enemy.

During Roman times it was considered good luck for a bride to wear a wreath of verbena blossoms—but only if she gathered the flowers herself. Romans also thought that he who wore verbena blossoms would be blessed with the gift of prophecy. Messengers with peaceful tidings often carried verbena with them.

Medieval times found men using verbena for protection against witches. Druids thought so highly of the plant that they offered a sacrifice to the earth before gathering it. The Saxons considered it protection against hail storms.

Verbena has been used extensively as medicine through the ages. It was used to cure scrofula, to treat the bites of rabid animals, and to prevent poisoning. Leaves, boiled in vinegar, were used to treat pleurisy, lumbago, and rheumatism. Sniffing dried, crushed leaves was thought to cure a headache. Concoctions made from the plant were also used to treat nerves, epilepsy, and asthma and were thought to strengthen the womb of a pregnant woman.

Superstition suggested that verbena, tied with one yard of white satin ribbon and left with a sick person, would hasten the return of good health.

Verbena has been called simple's joy because it was used so extensively for healing. An ancient meaning for the word *simple* is a medicinal plant or herb. The genus name, *Verbena*, is from *herbena*, from the two Latin words *herba* and *bona*, meaning "good plant."

Albartus Magnus, in his book *The Vertues of Herbes, Stones and Certain Beastes*, says that "infants bearing it (verbena) shall be very apte to learn and loving learninge, they shall be glad and joyous." Verbena was often used as an aphrodisiac, and people would sometimes stuff their pillows with dried verbena leaves for this purpose. Brides in Germany were offered wreaths or a love potion made of verbena blossoms. Dried blossoms were often strewn on the bedchamber floor. An infusion made from verbena blossoms and sprinkled over the floor in the dining room was thought to make the guests merrier.

In Hungary the plant was called lock-opening herb. Superstition held that if a thief made a cut on the palm of his hand and inserted a piece of verbena leaf in it, when the cut healed, he would have the power to open bolts and locks with a touch of his hand.

# FLORAL CALENDAR

Poinsettia — DECEMBER
Carnation — JANUARY
Chrysanthemum — NOVEMBER
Primrose — FEBRUARY
Calendula — OCTOBER
Violet — MARCH
Morning Glory — SEPTEMBER
Daisy — APRIL
Gladiolus — AUGUST
Lily-of-the-Valley — MAY
Water Lily — JULY
Rose — JUNE

# Floral Calendar

Calendars have existed for thousands of years in various forms. The Chinese, Japanese, Romans, Egyptians, and Hopi and Navajo Indians, among countless others, developed calendars. Each of these calendars was different, but each was an accurate means of keeping track of the seasons and the passage of time.

Because calendars were so closely tied with nature, it followed logically that different months should be associated with particular plants and flowers.

The Chinese, especially, used plants to keep track of time. According to Chinese folklore, two trees grew at the Court of Yao. One tree put forth one leaf every day for fifteen days as the moon waxed, and then it shed one leaf every day for fifteen days, as the moon waned. In this way they measured the months.

On the other side of the garden was a tree that put forth leaves every month for six months, then shed leaves every month for six months. In this way they kept up with the passage of the years.

A Chinese legend dating back to the seventh century A.D. says that Ho Hsien-ku, daughter of a humble shopkeeper, ate the peach of immortality given to her by Canopus, god of longevity. She then became one of the eight Taoist immortals and decreed that honor should be paid to a particular flower each month of the year. This formed the basis of the Chinese floral calendar.

Through the centuries, other civilizations adopted the custom of using a floral calendar. Primary among these were the Japanese and English.

The English took the art of keeping time with plants to an extreme with their experiments with a floral clock. A pet project of Carl Linnaeus, the floral clock, or watch of Flora, never worked quite as well as he had wished.

The basis of the clock was forty-six flowers that opened during different times of the day and night. This was complicated by the fact that different flowers stayed open different lengths of time. Further complications involved variations in temperature, moisture, and light intensity, which also caused the plants to open sooner or later than they were supposed to.

Another problem was that these flowers were chosen for when they opened, and not for their beauty or how they looked together. This created a garden that had little aesthetic appeal. Still another problem was that many of the flowers were of the Compositae family and had similar flower forms, giving a monotonous look to the garden.

Some of the flowers used were chicory, day lily, calendula, and sow thistle. One of the more reliable plants was *Tragopogon partensis*, Jack-go-to-bed-at-noon. This was thought to be so accurate that boys working in the fields based their lunch time on the movement of this flower.

In addition to formal calendars using certain flowers, superstitions and old wives' tales about plants and flowers abound for each month of the year. These are generally connected with the changes in weather and how they affect the gardener.

**January**:
    Chinese - plum blossom
    Japanese - pine
    English - carnation
"If the sun shines on New Year's Day, the flax will be straight."
"If the grass does grow in Janiveer, it grows the worse for it all the year."

**February**:
    Chinese - peach blossom
    Japanese - plum blossom, symbol of
                 longevity

English - primrose
"If Candlemas Day (February 2) be fair and bright, winter will have another flight."

**March**:

> Chinese - tree peony, symbol of love and affection
> Japanese - cherry blossom
> English - violet

"So many misties in March, so many frosties in May."

**April**:

> Chinese - cherry blossom, symbol of feminine principal
> Japanese - wisteria
> English - daisy

"April showers bring May flowers."
"When April blows his horn, 'tis good for both hay and corn."

**May**:

> Chinese - magnolia, symbol of feminine sweetness
> Japanese - iris
> English - lily of the valley

"If the weather be fine on the last day of May, the mowers may look for abundance of hay."

**June**:

> Chinese - pomegranate, symbol of progeny and posterity
> Japanese - peony
> English - rose

"It will be a wet summer if a cuckoo should be heard after June twenty-first."

**July**:

> Chinese - lotus flower, symbol of perfection and purity
> Japanese - mountain clover
> English - water lily

"If ant hills are high during July, the coming winter will be quite harsh."

**August**:

> Chinese - pear blossom, symbol of purity
> Japanese - the crest of a hill and the rising moon
> English - gladiolus

"If the twenty-fourth of August be fair and clear, then hope for a prosperous autumn that year."
"To smell wild thyme will renew spirits and energy in long walks under an August sun."

**September**:

> Chinese - mallow blossom
> Japanese - chrysanthemum
> English - morning glory

"September blows soft, till the fruit's in the loft."
"Trees planted on Saint Michaelmas Day (September 29) will grow quickly."

**October**:

> Chinese - chrysanthemum, symbol of harvest and rest
> Japanese - maple
> English - calendula

**November**:

> Chinese - gardenia
> Japanese - willow
> English - chrysanthemum

"If there's ice in November that will bear a duck, there'll be nothing after but sludge and muck."
"Onion skin very thin, mild winter's coming in; onion's skin thick and tough, coming winter cold and rough."

**December**:

> Chinese - poppy
> Japanese - paulownia
> English - poinsettia

"In December keep yourself warm and sleep."

# LANGUAGE OF THE FLOWERS

**PHLOX**
Sweet dreams

**IRIS**
Wisdom

Ever-lasting love

Faith
Valor
Comfort

**TULIP**
The perfect love

**DAFFO-DIL**
Regard

**LILY**
Hatred

**ROSE**
RED

Desire
Love

WHITE
Majesty

**PANSY**
Recollection

**DAISY**
Innocence
Gentleness

slc

# Names and Meanings of Flowers

Floral communication is at least as old as the Golden Age of Greece. According to Greek and Roman myths, many gods, goddesses, and innocent nymphs were transformed into various flowers which, in turn, took on the characteristics of these personages. For example, narcissus is named for the Greek youth who spent his days looking at his own reflection, and now this plant is a symbol of egotism. Another example is of hyacinth, which, the myths tell us, grew out of the blood of Hyacinthus, a young man who loved sports and games. Hyacinth is now a symbol of sports, games, and play.

The Greeks used flowers extensively in their ceremonies and in their day-to-day lives. Though they apparently conveyed messages by sending different flowers in a bouquet or garland, we can only guess which flowers had which meanings for them.

Floral symbols seem to have been used by the early Chinese, Assyrians, Egyptians, and Indians. According to *The Mystery and Magic of Trees and Flowers*, by Lesley Gordon, the first mention of English floral symbols was during the reign of Elizabeth I (1533–1603.) William Hunnis, an English poet, wrote verses that included the phrases "gillyflowers is for gentleness," and "marigolds is for marriage," and "cowslips is for council."

It was the Turks in the late seventeenth century who truly developed the art of communicating with flowers. They could convey almost any sentiment using different flowers. Displeasure, love, compassion, forgiveness, friendship, and countless other feelings could be sent by means of a bouquet of flowers.

The language of flowers was introduced to England in the early 1700s by Lady Mary Wortley Montagu, wife of the English ambassador to Turkey. On March 16, 1718, Lady Montagu wrote to a friend in England telling her that the "fair maidens of the East have lent a mute speech to flowers."

Enthralled with this custom, Lady Montagu published her *Turkish Letters* in 1763, explaining the floral symbolism for many different kinds of flowers. The custom caught on and appealed to romantics throughout the country. In the early 1800s the poet Thomas Hood wrote that "sweet flowers alone can say what passion fears revealing."

## The Victorian Language of Flowers

The language of flowers was quite suited to Victorian England, for it allowed for communication between lovers without the knowledge of ever-present chaperons and parents. Messages that would be a social impossibility if spoken could be conveyed by sending certain types of flowers. How these flowers were sent was of great importance as well, for this was also part of the message. If the blossom was presented upright, it carried a positive thought. If the flower came upside down, it might mean quite the opposite. If the giver intended the message to refer to himself, he would incline the flower to the left. If the message referred to the recipient, it would be inclined toward the right.

If flowers were used to answer a question and were handed over with the right hand it meant "yes"; with the left hand the answer was "no." Other conditions of the plant were important as well.

For example, if a boy sent a girl a rosebud with the leaves and thorns still on it, it meant "I fear, but I hope." If the rosebud was returned upside down, it meant, "you must neither fear nor hope." If the rosebud was returned with the thorns removed, the message was "you have everything to hope for." If the thorns were left but the leaves removed, the message was "you have everything to fear." If the young lady kept the rosebud and placed it in her hair, it meant "caution." If she placed it over her heart, the message was clearly "love."

The Victorians took the language of flowers a bit further and actually began attributing personalities to various flowers, as Thomas Hood exemplified:

The cowslip is a country wench,
The violet is a nun;—
But I will woo the dainty rose
The queen of everyone.

During the last part of the nineteenth century, several floral dictionaries were published. Among these were *The Poetical Language of Flowers* (1847), *The Language and Sentiments of Flowers* (1857), *The Floral Telegraph* (1874), and Kate Greenaway's *The Language of Flowers*, first published in 1884 and republished in 1978.

Because more than one dictionary existed, the possibility for error was great. One of these floral misinterpretations was made famous by Louisa Anne Twamley in her poem "Carnations and Cavaliers." The poem describes how a knight gave his lady a pink rose, meaning our love is perfect happiness. His lady either did not know about the language of flowers or did not care, for she sent back to him a carnation, which means refusal. The result was tragedy: the lovers died for each other's love.

It was during the Victorian period that tussie-mussies became popular. A tussie-mussie is a small bouquet of fresh or dried flowers, usually surrounded by lacy doilies and satin ribbons. Tussie-mussies were popular, in part, for the very practical purpose of warding off bad smells and disease. Some of the most useful flowers for this purpose included lavender, rosemary, and thyme.

Tussie-mussies made marvelous gifts then, and they still do. They are easy to make and, accompanied by a card explaining the meanings of the flowers used, make a uniquely personal present.

Tussie-mussies can be made from either fresh or dried flowers. Choose a relatively large, perfect blossom for the center flower. A perfectly formed rose blossom is wonderful for this. Surround this with smaller blossoms and ferns and put the stems through a doily or starched lace. If using fresh flowers, wrap the stems with damp paper towels and then cover them with plastic wrap or foil held in place with florist tape. If using dried flowers, simply wrap the stems with florist tape.

Fresh flowers that are good to use in tussie-mussies include rose, baby's breath, cornflower, phlox, aster, and carnation. Suitable dried flowers include strawflower, statice, honesty, ageratum, and sedum.

## Flowers and Their Meanings

**alyssum, sweet**: worth beyond beauty
**amaranth, globe**: immortality, unfading love
**amaryllis**: pride
**anemone, garden**: forsaken
**aster**: elegance and daintiness, talisman of love
**bachelor's button**: celibacy
**begonia**: beware! I am fanciful
**bellflower (white)**: gratitude
**bluebell**: constancy, delicacy, and humility
**carnation (pink)**: floral emblem of Mother's Day
**carnation (purple)**: antipathy and capriciousness
**carnation (red)**: admiration
**carnation (striped)**: refusal
**carnation (white)**: pure and ardent love, good-luck gift to woman
**carnation (yellow)**: disdain
**Christmas rose**: relieve my anxiety
**chrysanthemum (red)**: I love
**chrysanthemum (white)**: truth
**chrysanthemum (yellow)**: slighted love

**clematis**: mental beauty, ingenuity

**cockscomb**: affectation

**columbine**: cuckoldry and deserted lover, bad-luck gift to man

**columbine (purple)**: resolved to win

**columbine (red)**: anxious and trembling

**coreopsis**: always cheerful

**crocus**: abuse not

**crocus, spring**: youthful gladness

**crocus, saffron**: mirth

**cyclamen**: diffidence, bad-luck gift to woman

**daffodil**: regard

**dahlia**: instability

**daisy**: innocence, gentleness

**daisy, garden**: I share your sentiments

**day lily**: coquetry

**fern**: fascination

**fern, maidenhair**: discretion

**flax**: domestic industry

**forget-me-not**: true love, forget me not

**foxglove**: insincerity

**frittilary, crown**: majesty, power

**fuschia**: taste, amiability

**geranium**: folly and stupidity

**geranium, scarlet**: comforting

**geranium, wild**: piety

**gladiolus**: you pierce my heart

**heliotrope**: devotion

**hibiscus**: delicate beauty

**hollyhock**: ambition

**honesty**: honesty

**hyacinth**: sport, game, play

**impatiens**: refusal and severed ties

**iris**: message, faith, wisdom, and valor

**iris, German**: flame

**jasmine (white)**: amiability

**jasmine (yellow)**: timidity and modesty

**larkspur**: open heart and ardent attachment

**lily (orange)**: hatred

**lily (white)**: sincerity and majesty

**lily of the valley**: purity and humility

**marigold**: disquietude and jealousy

**morning glory**: farewell and departure

**narcissus**: egotism and conceit

**nasturtium**: conquest and victory in battle

**pansy**: thoughtful recollection

**peony**: healing

**petunia**: anger and resentment

**phlox**: sweet dreams and proposal of love

**poppy**: eternal sleep and oblivion

**primrose**: early youth and young love

**rose (pink)**: our love is perfect happiness

**rose (red)**: love and desire

**rose (white)**: charm and innocence

**rose (white and red)**: unity

**rose (yellow)**: infidelity and jealousy

**rosebud**: beauty and youth

**rose, withered**: fading beauty, reproach

**Saint John's wort**: suspicion and superstition

**sedum**: lover's wreath

**snapdragon**: presumption and desperation

**snowdrop**: hope and consolation

**sunflower**: homage and devotion

**sweet pea**: departure and adieu

**tiger lily**: wealth and pride

**tuberose**: dangerous pleasures

**tulip**: symbol of the perfect lover

**verbena**: may you get your wish

**violet**: modesty and simplicity

**wallflower**: friendship in adversity

**yarrow**: disputes and quarrels

**zinnia**: thoughts of absent friends

## Botanical Names

The Victorian language of flowers is sometimes easier to understand than the botanical nomenclature that is assigned to every plant. This method of naming is based on the work done by Carolus Linnaeus (1707–1778), who established three categories: genus, species, and varieties. Most of these names are from Latin, though other languages are represented as well. Although the common names are undoubtedly more fun to use and perhaps easier to remember, the botanical names are indispensable for precise and efficient communication about plants.

Many of the botanical names are based on quirks and characteristics of the plants, or on where (or by whom) they were first found growing. The following is a list of commonly used species names and their meanings.

**africanus**:  of Africa
**agrarius**:  of the fields
**agustus**:  majestic or noble
**albus**:  white
**allianthus**:  with beautiful flowers
**alpinus**:  of the mountains
**amoenus**:  pleasing
**annuus**:  annual
**aurantiacus**:  orange colored
**aureus**:  golden
**belladonna**:  beautiful lady
**bellus**:  beautiful

**biennis**:  biennial
**biflorus**:  twinned flower
**caeruleus**:  dark blue
**campestris**:  of the fields
**canadensis**:  of Canada
**coccinea**:  scarlet
**elegans**:  elegant
**flava**:  yellow
**fragilis**:  fragile
**grandiflora**:  large flowered
**japonica**:  of Japan
**nobilis**:  of fine appearance
**officinalis**:  used in the apothecary shop
**patens**:  spreading
**purpurea**:  purple
**repens**:  creeping
**splendens**:  showy
**tinctoria**:  used by dyers

# Color in the Garden

Many factors contribute to the beauty of a flower. Its form, texture, fragrance, and intricate detail all add to its loveliness. Ask anyone to describe a flower, however, and the first thing mentioned is likely to be the color of the blossoms.

Not only does each flower have its own personality based on its history and usage, but different colors of the same flower will also connote different personalities. According to the Victorian language of flowers, white flowers tend to symbolize purity and innocence, while yellow flowers denote a negative feeling. The red rose symbolizes ardent love; the pink suggests a softer and more innocent emotion.

Consider the emotions evoked by different colors when planning a flower garden. Bright colors should be placed toward the front of the border, allowing the softer and more subtle shades to recede into the background. Use colors such as reds, oranges, and bright yellows in areas where activity will occur, near a children's play yard, or by a swimming pool. Save softer colors for quiet areas—a bench along a woodland path, perhaps. Flower colors do more than contribute to a mood. In many instances, they set the mood.

Nearly everyone has a favorite color, and the psychology of color preference has become quite a sophisticated science.

Certain traits and characteristics are common to most people who share a favorite color. Though not everyone can successfully wear the colors he or she likes best, what better place to "show your true colors" than in the garden? The flower color you choose to surround yourself with might reveal much about your personality.

## Red

Choose a great deal of red for your garden and you are probably an extrovert and impossible to ignore. You are enthusiastic and prone to impulsive moods and actions. Red is such a passionate color that it must be used carefully in the garden, perhaps as an accent or as a motif in a large area. Red blends well with white and yellow flowers or with gray foliaged plants. Without the benefit of other colored blossoms, red flowers look wonderful against a background of dark evergreens. Fences or walls in a red garden should be painted a stark white.

Love red and you might choose some of the following plants for your garden: canna lily, chrysanthemum, clematis, dahlia, dianthus, flax, geum, gladiolus, hollyhock, larkspur (red), Maltese cross, nasturtium, Oriental poppy, peony, petunia, phlox, potentilla, red-hot poker, rose, salvia, snapdragon, stock, tulip, yarrow, zinnia.

## Blue

Gardeners seem to be always looking for blue garden flowers. Not only does blue look spectacular outdoors, but as cut flowers, shades of blue and violet add great beauty indoors. Blue is most often chosen as a favorite color. A preference for blue indicates introspection, sensitivity, and conservatism. You tend to weigh your options carefully and are cautious about taking action.

In the garden blue is easy to blend with other colors. It goes particularly well with yellow, white, or pale gray foliage. Alone, however, it will get lost against a backdrop of evergreens.

Blue flowers to include within the garden are: ageratum, aster, balloon flower, bellflower, columbine, delphinium, flax (blue), forget-me-not, gentian, glory of the snow, grape hyacinth, hyacinth, iris, lupine, morning glory, petunia, phlox, primrose, sage (blue), scilla, vinca, violet.

White for a simple life · Naïveté & Innocence

Pink · Charm & warmth in personality

Introspection, sensitivity favors blue

Yellow · Imagination, intellect, ideals

Red suggests passion, impulse, enthusiasm

COLOR in the GARDEN

## Yellow

Those who love yellow will find that it contrasts well with red or blue. Many consider blue and yellow the most beautiful of all color combinations in the garden. If you love yellow, you have great imagination and a tremendous drive for self-fulfillment. Yellow is often chosen by intellects and idealists. You make a good confidante and a true friend.

Flowers in shades of yellow are abundant. Among the most popular are: allium, basket of gold, calendula, canna lily, chrysanthemum, clematis, columbine, coreopsis, cosmos, dahlia, daisy, day lily. gaillardia, gazania, gerber daisy, geum, gladiolus, globe flower, hyacinth, iris, marigold, narcissus, nasturtium, nicotiana, pansy, petunia, portulaca, potentilla, primrose, rose, Saint John's wort, sedum, snapdragon, strawflower, sunflower, tulip, violet, wallflower, winter jasmine, yarrow, zinnia.

## Pink

Many consider pink the finest of all garden colors. Lacking the passion of red but warmer than the cool blues, pink seems to take the best characteristics of all other colors. A love of pink indicates wealth, a good position in society, and a character full of charm and warmth. Those who love pink are usually pampered, loved, and cared for.

In the garden pink flowers can be successfully blended with pale blue or pale yellow flowers or plants with pale gray foliage. Architectural features such as fences or walls should be light gray or white.

For the "pink of perfection" plant: ageratum, anemone, aster, astilbe, baby's breath, balloon flower, begonia, bleeding heart, candytuft, Christmas rose, chrysanthemum, clematis, cleome, colchicum, coral bells, cornflower, cosmos, dahlia, day lily, foxglove, geranium, gladiolus, hibiscus, hollyhock, impatiens, morning glory, peony, pink, poppy, purple coneflower, scilla, sedum, snapdragon, spiderwort, stock, sweet pea, tulip, vinca, yarrow, zinnia.

## White

White is the great ameliorator in the garden. It often comes between two colors that would otherwise clash. White flowers are often best enjoyed in the evening, for their fragrance is usually strongest then, and they seem to illuminate the garden. It is difficult to go wrong with white in the garden. It blends well with red, blue, purple, pinks, and yellows. White flowers look most spectacular by themselves against a backdrop of dark evergreen.

People seldom choose white as a favorite color. Those who do generally enjoy a simple life. A preference for white indicates naivete and innocence.

White flowers to include within the garden are: alyssum, aster, astilbe, baby's breath, balloon flower, begonia, bleeding heart, calla lily, candytuft, Christmas rose, chrysanthemum, clematis, cleome, cosmos, crocus, dahlia, daisy, four-o'clock, gazania, geranium, gladiolus, glory of the snow, grape hyacinth, hollyhock, hosta, hyacinth, impatiens, iris, jasmine, lily, lily of the valley, narcissus, pansy, peony, petunia, phlox, pink, poppy, primrose, rose, scilla, snapdragon, spiderwort, stock, tulip, vinca, wisteria, zinnia.

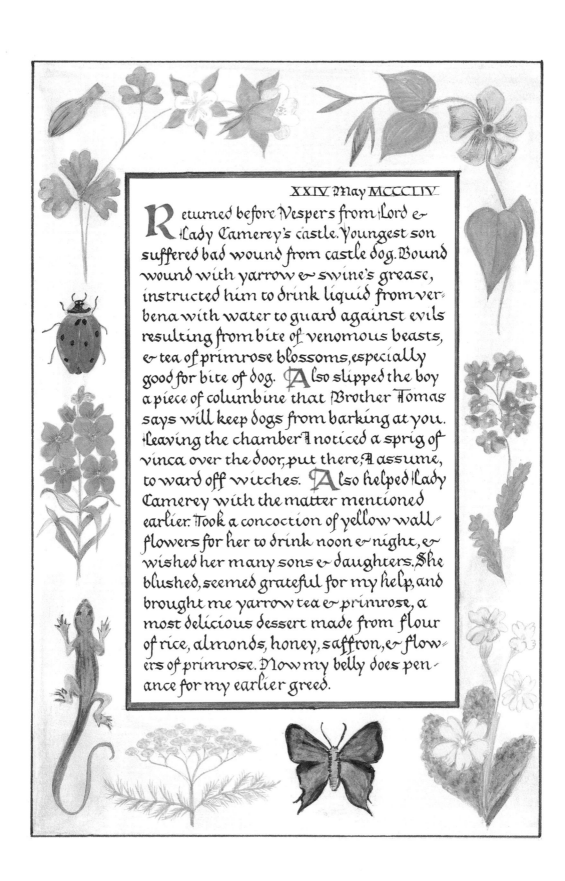

XXIV May MCCCLIV

Returned before Vespers from Lord & Lady Camerey's castle. Youngest son suffered bad wound from castle dog. Bound wound with yarrow & swine's grease, instructed him to drink liquid from verbena with water to guard against evils resulting from bite of venomous beasts, & tea of primrose blossoms, especially good for bite of dog. Also slipped the boy a piece of columbine that Brother Tomas says will keep dogs from barking at you. Leaving the chamber I noticed a sprig of vinca over the door, put there, I assume, to ward off witches. Also helped Lady Camerey with the matter mentioned earlier. Took a concoction of yellow wallflowers for her to drink noon & night, & wished her many sons & daughters. She blushed, seemed grateful for my help, and brought me yarrow tea & primrose, a most delicious dessert made from flour of rice, almonds, honey, saffron, & flowers of primrose. Now my belly does penance for my earlier greed.

# Gardens in History

With the fall of the Roman Empire, gardens for pleasure became, for a time, nonexistent. Gardens of the medieval period were utilitarian and could be categorized into kitchen gardens, containing herbs and flowers used for cooking, and physic gardens, in which were grown plants used in medicines and for healing. Flowers grown for their beauty were scarce and were used to decorate altars and shrines or to make wreaths or garlands worn by the priests on holy days.

## Medieval Gardens

Almost without exception, medieval gardens were based on strict geometrical shapes, usually squares or rectangles. They were always walled in or surrounded by thick hedges. Within these walls there was usually a rather large square or rectangular "flowery mede" filled with grass and a multitude of different flowers from the woods and fields. These were very similar to the meadow gardens that are so popular today. Both the word *meadow* and the word *mede* are from a root word meaning "mouth," for the medes were kept mown by the mouths of sheep and other grazing animals. These medes are often shown on medieval tapestries.

Other beds contained particular flowers or herbs for specific needs. These beds were raised above the normal soil level and were edged with planks. Rock or stone pathways separated the different beds. Along the walls or between the beds were raised hillocks covered with turf, used for sitting on during dry weather.

Some of the flowers included within medieval gardens were artemisia, autumn crocus, calendula, columbine, cornflower, crocus, English daisy, foxglove, hollyhock, iris, lavender, lily, lily of the valley, peony, poppy, primrose, rose, Saint John's wort, scilla, vinca, and wallflower.

## Colonial Gardens

Though separated by many centuries, colonial gardens and medieval gardens were similar in that they were both primarily utilitarian.

Early settlers in the New World had little time or energy to put into planting gardens for pleasure. Their gardens were, instead, an outgrowth of the needs of the colonists. Flowers grown were used for cooking, medicine, fragrance, and dyeing. There were really no typical colonial gardens, for each was based on the individual needs of a particular family. The plants in these gardens were grown from slips or seeds brought from the Old World, were given to the settlers by the Indians, or were transplanted from the surrounding woods and fields.

An additional function of these early gardens was to remind the colonists of the homes they had left behind and to help lessen the homesickness they felt. Familiar flowers and herbs helped them feel more at home.

Although gardens in Europe during this period were becoming more open and casual, the colonists were carving a new civilization out of wilderness, and they desired the strict geometry of a formal garden. Rigidly laid-out walks and beds with neat hedges not only made them feel more civilized, but also took less time to care for than freely formed spaces.

There was little organization as to placement of plants in these early American gardens. Vegetables, fruits, herbs, and flowers—all generally grew in the same plots. The "best" flowers were sometimes grown near the door to show them off or give them extra protection. Useful herbs were planted close to the kitchen door, where they were easily accessible.

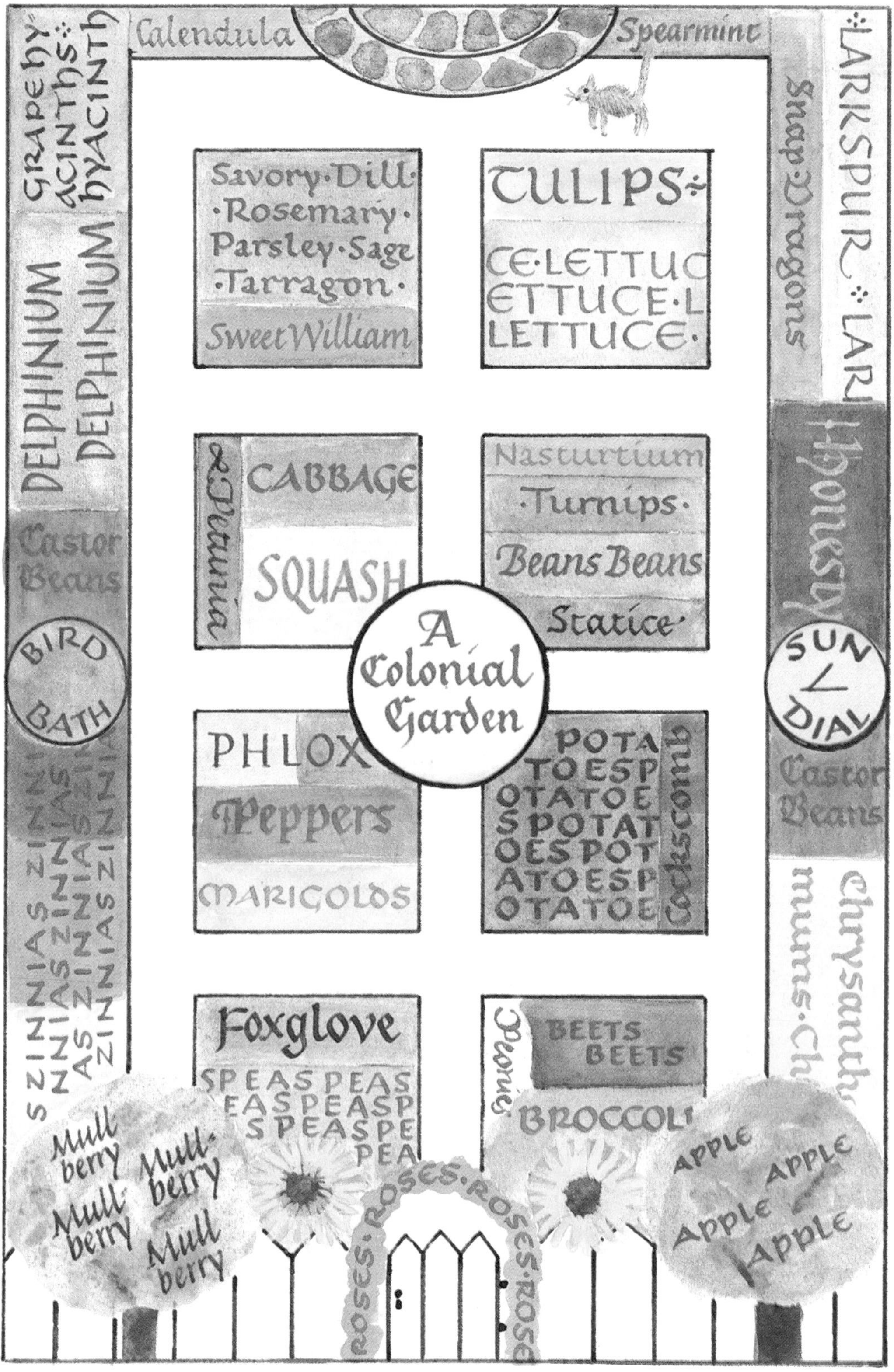

A Colonial Garden
Calendula
Spearmint
Grape hyacinths · hyacinth
Delphinium Delphinium
Castor Beans
Bird Bath
Zinnias
Larkspur
Snapdragons
Honesty
Sun Dial
Castor Beans
Chrysanthemums
Savory · Dill · Rosemary · Parsley · Sage · Tarragon ·
Sweet William
Tulips
Lettuce
Petunia
Cabbage
Squash
Nasturtium
· Turnips ·
Beans Beans
Statice
Phlox
Peppers
Marigolds
Potatoes
Cockscomb
Foxglove
Peas
Peonies
Beets Beets
Broccoli
Mullberry
Roses · Roses · Roses · Roses
Apple

Nearly all colonial gardens were surrounded by a fence. A picket fence was found to be the most useful, for it allowed good air circulation but kept animals out. Even the sharp points on the pickets had a purpose: they discouraged roosting fowls.

During the late colonial period, well-to-do gardeners planted landscapes imitating those popular in England. Broad sweeping lawns and manicured woods became a status symbol. Gardens planted in American cities at this time were very formal and were planted near the house so the family could enjoy both the beauty and the fragrance of the garden. Typically, these gardens consisted or eight square beds in the center with two wide borders parallel to the length of the fence. These beds would be separated by a series of gravel walks. Flowers found in colonial gardens included: calendula, Canterbury bells, day lily (yellow), globe flower, grape hyacinth, hollyhock, honesty, Johnny-jump-up, larkspur, nasturtium, peony, pink, tansy, tulip, and yarrow.

## Victorian Gardens

Love of flowers and gardening reached a passionate peak in the early 1800s in England. Queen Victoria came to the throne in 1837, and the mood of the times included a love of all things delicate and young and fresh. Flowers became an important part of the grand garden, and gardeners enthusiastically greeted new plants arriving from all over the world. Victorians were also passionately interested in scientific discoveries, and the art of flower hybridization was extremely popular.

With the rise of a new well-to-do middle class, the suburban garden was born. For the first time, businessmen worked in the city and lived in rural areas. Nicolette Scourse, in *The Victorians and Their Flowers*, said that "the suburban garden was acknowledged as a means by which a person could obtain social credit via his obvious wealth and his 'correct taste.'"

The feasibility of a suburban garden was increased dramatically with the invention of the lawn mower in 1830. Lawns had formerly been cut with a hand scythe or cropped by sheep. With a lawn mower, however, it was possible for a member of the middle class to maintain a grassy area without the help of gardeners and yard men or a flock of sheep.

Flower beds became a central point of the garden, and "bedding out" was quite the rage. This was the practice of setting out greenhouse plants during the summer months to add color to the garden. Used by the thousand, these flowers were sometimes arranged in designs and patterns.

Carpeting, the use of low-growing plants to add color, was also quite popular. Areas holding these floral carpets were sometimes sloped so that the viewer could better see the entire design.

With the Victorian passion for intrigue and clandestine meetings, secret paths and hidden benches became favorite parts of the garden. Grottoes, bowers, and ornate garden statuary completed the Victorian garden.

Toward the end of the nineteenth century, "bedding out" went out of vogue, and long perennial borders inspired by cottage gardens of rural England became popular.

Some of the flowers found in Victorian gardens were: aster, chrysanthemum, coreopsis, daffodil, delphinium, flax, hyacinth, Japanese iris, pincushion flower.

## Gardens Today

The utilitarian thrust of colonial and medieval gardens, and the ornate beauty of Victorian gardens, gives us the possibilities of landscapes to fill many individual needs. The most important thing about any garden is that it pleases its owner.

# FLOWERS USED FOR DYES

| COLOR | FLOWER | MORDANT |
|---|---|---|
| Crimson | ST. JOHN'S WORT | Vinegar |
| Red-orange | CALLIOPSIS | Chrome |
| Orange | DAHLIA (FLOWER) | Chrome |
| Orange | HOLLYHOCKS (FLOWER) | Chrome |
| Bronze | LILY·OF·THE·VALLEY (LEAVES) | Chrome |
| Light gold | GAILLARDIA (FLOWER) | Alum |
| Bright yellow | ZINNIA (FLOWER) | Alum |
| Yellow | MARIGOLD | Alum |
| Yellow-green | PURPLE ASTER (FLOWER) | Alum |
| Lime green | HOLLYHOCKS (LEAVES) | Alum |
| Green | LILY·OF·THE·VALLEY (LEAVES) | Alum |
| Blue-violet | PURPLE IRIS (BLOSSOM) | Chrome |
| Grey-black | YELLOW IRIS (ROOT) | Iron |

*See Appendix: Flowers in the Home, page 263, for more information on flowers for dyeing.*

COMMON NAME: **wisteria**
GENUS: *Wisteria*
SPECIES, HYBRIDS, CULTIVARS:
*W. sinensis*—Chinese; lilac blue.
*W. floribunda* 'Ivory Tower'—white; heavy bloom; discovered on campus of Princeton University. *W.* 'Rosea'—pink flowers.
*W.f.* 'Violacea Plena'—double blue flowers.
FAMILY: Leguminosae
BLOOMS: summer
TYPE: perennial
DESCRIPTION: A hardy, perennial vine, wisteria is covered with cascading flowers in long (15 to 20 inches) racemes. White, pink, and lilac blue colors are available. The vines can be grown over a fence, trellis, or wall, or can be trained into a standard—a form resembling a tree.
CULTIVATION: Wisteria needs a sunny spot and is very drought tolerant. Soils high in nitrogen might produce more foliage than blossoms. If flowering is poor, try a bit of selective pruning on the roots. Because of its vigorous growth habit, wisteria needs frequent pruning to keep it in check. Grown from seed, wisteria does not always stay true to the parent color.

Wisteria is a lovely, but aggressive, vine that has a honey-sweet scent. The white form produces a stronger scent than the more common purple variety. The plant has been reported as growing as much as 30 feet in a single growing season. The roots have been known to penetrate metal pipes and split open sewer and drain pipes.

The genus is a small one, containing only two species from the eastern United States and four species from the Far East. It was named by Thomas Nuttall in 1818 in honor of Casper Wistar, a German professor at the University of Pennsylvania. Until then it had been placed in the genus *Glycinia*

(from the Greek word *glykys*, meaning "sweet," because of the scent), and it is still sometimes referred to as glicine or glycine.

Chinese wisteria, *W. sinensis*, was brought to England from China in 1816. The English gardener who was a recipient of one of the first plants brought to Europe was said to have greatly mistreated the root. He inadvertently roasted it in his oven and then left it in a dark corner to freeze, yet the strong root remained viable and supplied him with a long-lasting, lovely plant once he actually got it planted in the ground.

The best species to grow as a standard is *W. floribunda*, brought from Japan in 1830.

Both the seeds and pods are poisonous, causing severe stomach cramps and pain. So potent are the toxins that it takes only a few seeds to poison.

COMMON NAME: **yarrow**

GENUS: *Achillea*

SPECIES, HYBRIDS, CULTIVARS:
*A. filipendulina* 'Gold Plate'—mustard yellow; 36 to 48 inches. *A.f.* 'Coronation Gold'—bright yellow flowers; 48 inches. *A. millefolium* 'Fire King'—deep red rose; 18 inches. *A. tomentosa*—wooly yarrow; dark green leaves; flower stems to 10 inches.

FAMILY: Compositae

BLOOMS: summer

TYPE: perennial

DESCRIPTION: Several kinds of yarrows range from very low growing, mat-forming species to very tall and stately plants. All yarrows have finely dissected fernlike leaves and tight clusters of flowers. Flower colors are yellow, white, red, pink, and cream.

CULTIVATION: Yarrow thrives in full sun and at least moderately well drained soil. Although established clumps will withstand long periods of drought, newly planted plants will survive and grow much better with ample moisture. Yarrow does not like too rich a soil and will form hardier, more sturdy plants if it is grown in poor to average soil. After the plant blooms, cut off the spent flower heads. Propagate yarrow by dividing clumps or by sowing ample numbers (because of its poor germination rate) of the seeds in spring.

This genus was named for Achilles, hero of Homer's *Iliad*, who was said to have given this plant to his soldiers to help stanch the flow of blood from their wounds during the Trojan War. Other common names reflect this blood-staunching characteristic of the plant. These include soldier's woundwort, nosebleed, bloodwort, staunchgrass, staunchweed, and sanguinary (from the Latin word for blood). Modern tests on the plant have found that it does indeed contain chemicals that help blood to clot. The leaves and flowers are sometimes drunk to fight fevers and to stimulate the appetite. The species name *millefolium* means "of a thousand leaves" and refers to the finely dissected leaves.

During the Middle Ages, yarrow was considered to have great medical and magical qualities and was sometimes called all heal. The Navajo Indians used it as a general tonic and for earaches, head colds, bruises, and burns. Sixteenth-century herbalist John Gerard wrote that chewing on a leaf would help a toothache.

Also called devil's plaything, yarrow was thought to have been used by the devil to cast evil spells. If wrapped in flannel and placed under the pillow, yarrow was supposed to cause one to dream of matters of love. To dream of cabbages under these circumstances, however, was sure to bring bad luck.

According to superstition, yarrow in the herb garden had the effect of stengthening aromatic oils of other herbs.

The Chinese believed that eating yarrow would brighten the eye and promote intelligence.

COMMON NAME: **zinnia**
GENUS: *Zinnia*
SPECIES, HYBRIDS, CULTIVARS:
*Z. elegans*: dahlia type, cactus type, bedding type
FAMILY: Compositae
BLOOMS: summer
TYPE: annual
DESCRIPTION: Plant hybridizers have worked magic on the original plain-Jane zinnia. This plant now exhibits tremendous diversity: it has blooms in every color except blue and ranges in height from 6 to 36 inches. Flower forms vary from single and simple to large, double varieties.
CULTIVATION: Zinnias thrive in heat and will not grow or flower very well when the weather is cool. Sow seeds outdoors after the soil has warmed. Good air circulation is important to prevent mildew. Water zinnias regularly, but do not overwater. Soaking the soil rather than watering by spraying will also help with the mildew problem.

When zinnias were introduced to European gardeners, they were received with no more enthusiasm than they had provoked in their own country. They were called everybody's flower and poorhouse flower because they were so easily grown and common looking.

One common name, garden Cinderella, alludes to the transformation that the zinnia underwent. In 1886 a French botanist produced the first double zinnia in bright colors, and in 1920 Luther Burbank produced the first dahlialike zinnia. Hybridization did wonders with this plain little flower until today the number of colors and flower forms available is staggering.

Another popular name for the plant is youth and old age, since the old flowers stay fresh as the new flowers open and begin to bloom.

This is the state flower of Indiana.

The zinnias that were found growing in the wilds of Mexico in 1519 were small with dingy purple or dull yellow blossoms. The Aztec Indian name for them was "eyesore," and they were essentially ignored.

Zinnia was named for Dr. Gottfried Zinn, an eighteenth-century German whose hobby was hybridizing wildflowers. A favorite story about Dr. Zinn tells how he was collecting plants in Mexico when he was attacked by bandits. All he had in his bag were the dried flower heads of wildflowers. When the bandits opened the bag and saw this they left him alone, for it was bad luck to attack the feeble-minded and who but a feeble-minded old man would carry around a bag of dead flowers?

# Fall

COMMON NAME:  **ageratum**
GENUS:  *Ageratum*
SPECIES, HYBRIDS, CULTIVARS:
*A. houstonianum.* Blue hybrids: Blue
Blazer, Blue Angel, Blue Mink, Blue Surf,
Midget Blue, Florist's Blue. White: Album,
Summer Snow, Mexican White. Purple: Royal
Blazer. Pink: Fairy Pink, Pinkie.
FAMILY:  Compositae
BLOOMS:  summer and fall
TYPE:  annual
DESCRIPTION:  Ageratum hybrids vary
in height from 5 to 24 inches. Their spread is
generally 6 to 9 inches. Individual flowers
are clustered tightly and resemble small
powder puffs.
CULTIVATION:  Seeds should be sown
in the garden in early May. Press the seeds
firmly into the seedbed, but do not cover
them, for they need light to germinate. It
takes approximately ten days for the seeds to
germinate. To start seeds indoors, sow them
in March and allow the plants to become
well established (two to three sets of true
leaves) before you transplant them into the
garden. Ageratum will thrive in full sun or
partial shade.

Ageratum is also known as floss flower.
There are about forty-five species of
annual herbs in the genus, all native to South
America. Many species reseed easily and are
marvelous to include in a naturalized setting
for good fall color. Hybridized varieties are
often available in spring and are excellent to
use as bedding plants throughout spring and
summer and into fall.

———  ✿  ———

Ageratum is native to Central America. Its
attractive blooms last a long time before they
start to look old. This fact is reflected in the
name, which is from Greek words *a*,
meaning "not," and *geras* meaning "old." It
has also been suggested that to eat the flower
would keep a person from getting old.

Dwarf varieties of ageratum are
particularly popular as edging plants. Taller
varieties look spectacular with yellow
chrysanthemums in the fall garden.

COMMON NAME:  **anemone**
GENUS:  *Anemone*
SPECIES, HYBRIDS, CULTIVARS:
*A. hybrida* 'Queen Charlotte'—deep pink;
2½ to 3 feet. *A.h.* 'Honorine
Jobert'—white. *A.h.* 'September
Charm'—pink. *A. coronaria* 'Flore
Pleno'—double scarlet flowers.
FAMILY:  Ranunculaceae
BLOOMS:  fall
TYPE:  perennial
DESCRIPTION:  Flowers come in single
or double forms and in shades of pink, red,
and white, measuring 2 to 3 inches across.
The foliage looks like grape leaves.
Depending on the variety, the height may
vary from 8 inches to 3 feet. The plants form
attractive mounds that spread 1 to 2 feet.
Golden stamens are a beautifully conspicuous
part of this flower.
CULTIVATION:  Anemones need rich,
well-drained soil and plenty of moisture. In
cold regions, a light mulch will be helpful.
These plants do best in partial shade or
filtered sun, or in full sun in areas where the
summers do not get too hot. Anemone plants
should be set out during spring, or seeds can
be sown in spring. Plants are slow to get
established and should never need dividing.

A Greek legend tells of the origin of
anemone. This was the name of nymph who
was loved by Zephyr, the god of the West
Wind. Flora, goddess of the flowers, became
jealous and changed Anemone into a flower
that always bloomed before the return of
spring. Zephyr preferred her as a nymph and
abandoned her to Boreas, god of the North
Wind. Anemone never learned to love
Boreas, but he aroused her emotions so that
she always bloomed too early and faded too
quickly.

Another Greek myth said that the
anemones were formed from Venus's tears
when she cried over the body of Adonis.

The name anemone comes from the
Sanskrit word *anti*, which means "he
breathes." Pliny wrote that the anemones
would open only at the bidding of the wind.
In the Near East they were a symbol of
disease, and it was thought that the flowers
sometimes actually carried the disease. An
early European custom was to hold one's
breath while running past a field of
anemones, for the country folk felt that even
the air was poisoned from these flowers.
Luckily for us, this superstition quickly died
out.

The Egyptians, and later the English,
used these flowers as charms against disease
and often wore them around their necks or
arms.

The scarlet anemone, *A. coronaria*, was
thought to be representative of the scarlet
robes of Solomon. Some considered it to be
the lilies of the field mentioned in the Song
of Solomon. In Palestine this flower is
sometimes called "blood drops of Christ,"
for it was thought to have grown under the
cross. The species name comes from the fact
that these blossoms were often used in
wreaths, garlands, or crowns.

Robert Fortune, a nineteenth-century
plant explorer, found the Japanese anemone
(*A. japonica*) growing near Shanghai. The
species name is from the fact that this plant
grows profusely in Japan.

The story is told of a French botanist
who obtained anemone plants in the early
1600s. For ten years he refused to give or
sell any of these plants or the seeds they
produced. This situation lasted until a great
and famous plantsman came to visit the
Frenchman's garden and "dropped" his coat
on the seed-laden plants. When he picked it
up, many of the seeds stuck to his coat. He

took these seeds home, planted them, and very generously shared the plants and seeds that resulted.

According to the Victorian language of flowers, the wild anemone symbolizes brevity and expectation (for the flower blooms for such a short time), and the garden flower means forsaken, referring to the myth of its origin.

COMMON NAME: aster
GENUS: *Aster*
SPECIES, HYBRIDS, CULTIVARS:
Most hybrids were developed from
*A. Novae-belgii* and *A. Novae-angliae*.
'Eventide'—purple; 4 to 5 feet tall; from
*A. Novae-belgii*. 'Harrington's Pink'—light
pink; 5 feet tall; from *A. Novae-angliae*.
Dwarf forms also available.
FAMILY: Compositae
BLOOMS: fall
TYPE: annuals and perennials
DESCRIPTION: Small daisylike flowers
come in shades of pink, purple, and red.
Yellow centers contrast beautifully with the
colored ray flowers. Taller varieties grow to
be 36 to 56 inches tall. Dwarf varieties grow
as short as 8 inches.
CULTIVATION: Plants should be
divided in very early spring and replanted
immediately. Native species come very easily
from seed but might not stay true to the
color of the parent plant. Asters are
adaptable to varying environmental
conditions but perform best with full sun
and ample moisture.

Asters are ancient wildflowers that were
considered sacred to Greek and Roman
deities. Two myths told of the origin of the
asters. The first said that Virgo scattered
stardust on the earth, and the fields bloomed
with asters. The second said that the goddess
Asterea looked down upon the earth and saw
no stars. The sight saddened her so that she
began to cry, and where her tears fell, there
the asters bloomed.

Known as starwort in England and
Germany and as eye of Christ in France,
asters have always been thought to carry
magical powers. In ancient Greece, aster
leaves were burned to keep away evil spirits
and drive off serpents. Ointment made from
asters was supposed to cure the bite of a mad
dog.

Virgil wrote that asters boiled in wine
and placed near a beehive would improve
the flavor of the honey.

In 1637 John Tradescant, Jr., took native
asters from America and introduced them to
Europe. Europeans liked this wild member of
the daisy family and it soon became a
favorite garden flower. Two of the most
popular asters are the New England aster (*A.
Novae-angliae*) and New York aster (*A.
Novae-belgii*). The species name for New
York aster is "New Belgium" because New
York was originally called New Amsterdam;
the Dutch were the first to settle that area,
and Holland was at one time included in a
Roman province called Belgica.

Purple asters were often used to dye
wool a greenish gold color.

Aster is the flower chosen as the floral
emblem for September.

The popular Chinese asters are not true
asters but are in the genus *Callistephus*.
Jesuit missionaries found these plants
growing wild near Peking. They sent plants
back to Europe and since they resembled
asters from America, they were nicknamed
Chinese asters. Seeds from these plants were
sent to Paris in 1728, and the first plants
were grown at Versailles. They were soon
hybridized to produce double and even
quadruple florets. So enthusiastic were the
Germans about hybridizing this plant they
were sometimes known as German asters. By
1750 it was said that Chinese asters grew
from Scotland to the Rhine. They were
introduced to America in 1806.

Chinese aster comes in so many subtle
shades that it is a symbol of variety. It was
planted in Chinese gardens in pots with one
shade blending into another and was said to
look like a rainbow. The genus name is from
two Latin words, *kallistos*, meaning "most
beautiful," and *stephos*, meaning "crown."

COMMON NAME: **calendula**
GENUS: *Calendula*
SPECIES, HYBRIDS, CULTIVARS:
*C. officinalis* 'Golden Gem'—dwarf;
double; yellow. 'Pacific Beauty'—double;
yellow, orange, apricot; more heat tolerant
than other cultivars. 'Orange Gem'—double;
medium orange. 'Chrysantha'— double;
buttercup yellow.
FAMILY: **Compositae**
BLOOMS: summer and fall
TYPE: annual
DESCRIPTION: Calendulas have light
green aromatic leaves and large (up to 4
inches across), daisylike flowers that come in
shades of yellow and orange. Plants get to be
approximately 2 feet tall with a spread of 12
to 15 inches, though dwarf varieties that
grow only half that size are also available.
CULTIVATION: Calendula performs
best in cool weather and is often used as a
fall bedding plant. For fall bloom, the seeds
should be sown outdoors in mid-June. The
seeds, which should be sown $^1/_4$ inch deep,
germinate best at temperatures ranging from
75 to 85 degrees Fahrenheit. They need total
darkness, so be sure that all the seeds are
covered well. The plants need full sun but
can tolerate relatively poor soil.

Calendulas are often planted in the herb bed
because of their extensive medicinal and
culinary value. An ancient recipe using an
infusion of calendula blossoms in wine was
supposed to "soothe a cold stomach." Made
into a salve, calendula was used to cure
toothaches, jaundice, sore eyes, and skin
irritations. The flowers were also thought to
be good for measles, varicose veins, and
ulcers. Gerard, who wrote an English herbal,
suggested that a concoction made from the
flowers and sugar, taken in the morning,
would keep one from trembling. The plant

was also thought to draw "evil humours" out
of the head, strengthen eyesight, and protect
one from poisoning and angry words. The
juice, when mixed with vinegar, was used to
relieve swelling.

Calendula was used extensively as a
medicine during the Civil War and World
War I, when Gertrude Jekyll instigated a
campaign to grow and gather calendulas to
be used to dress wounds. They were shipped
to first-aid stations in France. Even today, the
petals, made into an ointment, are good for
oily skin.

Calendula was also used as seasoning.
The Romans used both leaves and flowers in
salads and preserves and as seasoning for
meats. The Saxons were thought to have
used the plant in place of salt and pepper.
Since that time, the flowers have been used
to season broths, wine, and other drinks.
The blossoms have also been pickled and
candied.

Today calendula is used to garnish
meats, in cream soups, and in stuffed eggs. It
is also added to egg dishes and fruit breads
(pumpkin, banana, and so on) for color and
delicate flavor. A delicious egg salad spread
can be made with hard-boiled eggs,
mayonnaise, and seasonings, including
chopped calendula petals. To eat calendula,
however, was supposed to make one feel
more amorous, see fairies, or be easily
induced to sleep.

The flowers were also popular in
nosegays and bouquets. In addition to their
beauty, the pungent odor of the flowers was
said to have been useful in keeping ladies
awake during long sermons.

Calendula played more important roles
in church as well. Early Christians put these
flowers by the statues of the Virgin Mary and
called them "Mary's gold." The bright yellow
flowers of calendula have been used as
decorations for temples and festivals
throughout the centuries. Called "herb of the
sun," calendula was considered the most

sacred herb of ancient India. Holy men of that country were said to have strung the blossoms into garlands and placed them around the necks of the gods.

Calendula was sometimes called summer's bride or husbandman's dial, for the flower head follows the path of the sun throughout the day. This plant is also called pot marigold, because it was commonly planted in big pots or flower beds. "The marigold goes to bed with the sun and with him rises weeping" refers to the fact that the flower heads close up during the night and the ray flowers, curved inward, trap dew inside. The genus name is from the Latin word *calendae*, which means "throughout the months" and refers to the extremely long blooming season that this plant enjoys in optimum growing conditions.

A native of southern Europe, calendula often escapes cultivation in southern California. This flower is the English floral emblem for the month of October.

Because of their stiff stems and large flowers, calendulas make excellent cut flowers and are often grown in the greenhouse during winter months for this purpose. The brightly colored petals make a good dye.

COMMON NAME: **chrysanthemum**
GENUS: *Chrysanthemum*
SPECIES, HYBRIDS, CULTIVARS:
The garden chrysanthemum,
*C. morifolium*, is a hybrid developed from
four species native to Asia. Many cultivars
have been developed from this one, differing
in size, shape, type of flowering head,
growth habit, color, and time of bloom.
FAMILY: **Compositae**
BLOOMS: fall
TYPE: perennial
DESCRIPTION: The many classes of
chrysanthemums include pompon, quill,
spider, brush, thistle, single, incurve, and
spoon. These classes are based on the
physical characteristics of the flowering
head.
CULTIVATION: Small chrysanthemum
plants can be purchased in spring, set in the
garden or holding bed throughout the
summer, and then put on display beginning
in early fall. The plants develop very shallow
root systems, so they can be transplanted
easily in late summer with few problems.

Conscientious pruning during early
summer will result in bushy plants with
numerous flowers. Pinch back new plants
when they are 6 inches tall, and continue to
pinch back the flowering stems until ninety
days before they bloom.

Chrysanthemums are heavy feeders.
They will benefit from weekly applications
of liquid manure or biweekly applications of
a quickly soluble fertilizer. Continue to
fertilize them until the buds begin to show
color.

Chrysanthemums are very ancient plants, as
supported by the fact that Confucius wrote
of them in 500 B.C. The ancient Chinese
botanist T'ao Ming-yang developed many
new strains of chrysanthemums so beautiful
that people came from great distances to
view them. Soon his village became known
as Chuh-sien, or the city of chrysanthemums.

Chrysanthemums were always great
favorites of the noble class, and in China, up
until a relatively short time ago, common
folk were not allowed to grow them in their
gardens.

Records show that chrysanthemum
seeds came to Japan by way of Korea in the
fourth century. In A.D. 910 Japan held its first
Imperial Chrysanthemum Show and declared
this the national flower.

Claire Haughton in her book *Green
Immigrants* tells the following legend of
how the chrysanthemum came to Japan: The
Empire of Japan was born when a shipload
of twelve maidens and twelve young men
from China set out to find the "herb of
youth," which kept people eternally young.
They carried baskets of chrysanthemums to
trade for this herb. After many weeks at sea,
their ship wrecked near an uninhabited
island. They swam to shore, planted the
chrysanthemums, and settled down to build
an empire. Japan's imperial coat of arms
shows a sixteen-petaled golden
chrysanthemum.

Chrysanthemums were first introduced
to Europe in 1688, and their reception there
was not enthusiastic. They were essentially
ignored for many years by most European
gardeners, despite the fact that records from
the 1700s indicate the Dutch were growing
at least six species. In 1843 the Royal
Horticultural Society sent Robert Fortune to
China to obtain the hardy autumn-flowering
chrysanthemums, and this seems to have
triggered great interest. By the mid-1800s
their popularity had been established.
Particularly popular in France were the small,
rounded varieties, which were called
pompons because of their similarity to the
small, wool pompons found on soldier's
hats.

Chrysanthemums were introduced to the

United States in 1798, and by 1850 many nurseries were carrying as many as forty varieties. In 1900 the Chrysanthemum Society of America was established, and they staged their first exhibit in 1902 in Chicago.

The genus name is from two descriptive Latin words, meaning "yellow" and "flower." These flowers make a very good dye.

In the Victorian language of flowers, this plant means cheerfulness and optimism. The Chinese consider it a sign of rest and ease, and the Japanese take it as a sign of long life and happiness. According to the Japanese floral calendar, it is the flower of September. The English calendar claims it for November.

Chrysanthemum petals are quite tasty and are particularly good added to cream soups or various salads (including green, fruit, or chicken). Blanch the petals for several seconds before using them, but don't cook them too long as this makes them bitter.

COMMON NAME: colchicum
GENUS: *Colchicum*
SPECIES, HYBRIDS, CULTIVARS:
*C. speciosum. C. autumnale*
'Alba'—white. *C.a.* 'Majus'—large.
*C.a.* 'Minus'—dwarf form. *C.a.*
'Roseum'—rose pink.
FAMILY: Liliaceae
BLOOMS: fall
TYPE: perennial
DESCRIPTION: The flowers are lavender, red, or rose colored. They resemble crocus blooms and can be either single or double forms. The blossoms appear in fall but the leaves don't appear until spring and they die back by midsummer.
CULTIVATION: Plant the corms in late summer or early fall, as soon as they are available from a garden center. They should be planted 3 to 4 inches deep and 6 to 9 inches apart in sun or partial shade. Additional plants can be obtained by digging the corms in midsummer when the leaves have died back, separating the corms, and replanting them immediately.

Many nicknames have been given to colchicum based on its similarity to crocus blossoms: autumn crocus, fall crocus, meadow crocus, and meadow saffron (referring to *Crocus sativus*, the source of saffron). Names like naked ladies have been assigned to it because of its unusual growth pattern—flowers appearing without the leaves. Because the flowers seemed to bloom magically without help from green leaves, the names mysteria and wonder bulb were also given to colchicum.

The genus name, *Colchicum*, refers to Colchis, an ancient region on the Black Sea, where these flowers grew in great profusion. It was here that Greek mythology says Medea used her magical powers to restore youth to her favorites and poison her enemies with the roots of colchicum. Variations of this legend say that the colchicums grew where Medea spilled drops of a magic concoction, or that the plant is named for Medea herself who, like the colchicums, was beautiful but poisonous.

The corms of colchicum contain alkaloids and were well known for their poisonous properties. Slaves in Greece were said to have eaten just enough of the corms to cause themselves to be too sick to work but not sick enough to be dangerously ill. Sufficient quantities were thought to be lethal, and the powdered roots of colchicum, mixed with alcoholic beverages, were given to many an unsuspecting victim. Discorides, an ancient Roman writer, said that it "killeth by choking" though it is "strangely alluring due to its pleasantness." Bulbs from wild plants are thought to be more poisonous than those from cultivated varieties.

As with many other poisonous plants, correct amounts mixed with the right ingredients were effectively used for medicines. Colchicum corms have been used to treat diseases since the time of the pharaohs. During the Renaissance, people often wore bulbs from this plant around their necks to ward off infection in times of plague. During medieval times, a concoction made from these flowers and water was used to improve a woman's complexion. More recently, juice from the corms has been used to treat gout.

Linnaeus wrote of many uses of colchicum, including ridding men and animals of fleas, coloring Easter eggs, and dyeing fishing nets green.

Today botanists are excited about the potential of a drug called colchine that can be extracted from colchicum corms. This drug can change sterile hybrids to fertile ones, which could have a tremendous effect on plant breeding.

COMMON NAME: **sedum**

GENUS: *Sedum*

SPECIES, HYBRIDS, CULTIVARS:
*S. kamtschaticum*—3 to 4 inches tall; orange or yellow blooms. *S. sieboldii*—silver green leaves; pink flowers on 6- to 9-inch stems. *S. spectabile*—18 inches tall; carmine red flowers. *S. telephium* 'Autumn Joy'—rosy pink flowers on 18- to 24-inch stems.

FAMILY: Crassulaceae

BLOOMS: fall

TYPE: perennial

DESCRIPTION: Sedums generally have thick, fleshy leaves and stems. The flower heads are composed of masses of tiny, star-shaped flowers. The most popular of the sedums are *S. spectabile* and *S. telephium*, both producing pink to dark red flowers.

CULTIVATION: Plant sedums in full sun and well-drained soil. Many of the low-growing varieties make excellent rock garden plants. Though they tolerate neglect and poor soil, sedums will repay you handsomely for a little tender loving care, which should include regular watering. When plants become crowded after four to five years, divide and replant them in early spring.

This genus comprises at least 250 species, which are native to many different areas. The genus is characterized by remarkable diversity and a wide range of environmental tolerances. There are sedums that are mat forming, growing only a few inches tall, and there are some sedums that produce beautiful, large blossoms reaching 3 to 4 feet. Some are annuals, some perennials; some are grown only for their bloom, others just for their foliage.

The name sedum dates back to the time of the Romans, who grew this plant on their roofs to keep away lightning. The name comes from the Latin word *seob*, which means "to calm" or "allay."

# Winter

COMMON NAME: **amaryllis**
GENUS: *Amaryllis*
SPECIES, HYBRIDS, CULTIVARS:
*A. belladonna* 'Appleblossom'—pink and
white. *A.b.* 'Dazzler'—white with light
green tones. *A.b.* 'Liberty'—crimson.
FAMILY: Amaryllidaceae
BLOOMS: winter
TYPE: perennial
DESCRIPTION: Amaryllis blossoms are
truly spectacular. They form on sturdy
20-inch stems and then produce explosions
of color, sometimes as many as five blossoms
to a stem. Colors range from white to pink,
red, salmon, and orange, with color
combinations on the blossoms of many
species.
CULTIVATION: Considered very easy to
grow, amaryllis is usually grown indoors as a
potted plant. Potted bulbs should be kept on
the dry side so that the leaves come after the
flower scapes appear, resulting in delayed
bloom time. According to White Flower Farm
catalog, blossoms will last longer if the
anthers are removed as soon as the plant
opens. If the anthers are already losing
pollen, it is too late to use this trick.

Amaryllis is extremely poisonous. Many of
the South American Indian tribes used the
sap from the plant to make poisonous
arrows. The name *Amaryllis* is from the
Greek word *amarullis*, which means "to
shine." Virgil wrote of a young shepherd boy
serenading his love, the shepherdess
Amaryllis. During the Renaissance, amaryllis
referred to certain dances and madrigals.

COMMON NAME: **Christmas rose**
GENUS: *Helleborus*
SPECIES, HYBRIDS, CULTIVARS:
*H. niger* 'Angustifolius'—small flowering,
pure white form. *H.n.* 'Praecox'—blooms
September–February. *H.n.* 'Major.'
*H.n.* 'Multiflorus'—smaller flowers.
FAMILY: Ranunculaceae
BLOOMS: winter
TYPE: perennial
DESCRIPTION: This plant, which
grows to a height of 12 to 18 inches, has
interesting evergreen leaves that are slightly
toothed and divided into seven to nine
leaflets. The large white flowers are 2 inches
or more across, with bright yellow stamens
in the center. The blossoms turn pink or
purplish as they age.
CULTIVATION: Christmas roses prefer
sandy, neutral soil rich in humus. They do
best with a bit of winter chill, and they need
heavy mulch to protect them from summer
heat. Protection from winter storms and
severe weather will also benefit the plants.
Winter sun, summer shade, and ample
moisture throughout the year are the perfect
conditions for the Christmas rose. Plants can
be divided in late summer, or after flowering,
and planted immediately. Plant new plants in
fall or spring, approximately 18 inches apart.
It will take a year or so for these plants to
get established and bloom well. Established
clumps should be treated to a top dressing of
compost or liquid fertilizer in February.
Although the Christmas roses have a
reputation for being somewhat introverted
and wanting to be left alone, garden writer
Vita Sackville-West contends that this
reputation is not "wholly deserved: If the
plant is dug with a large ball of soil, it will
transplant quite easily."

———— ✍ ————

Christmas rose, also commonly known as
hellebore, provides a delightful bit of spirit
for the winter garden and deserves the
attention it gets due to the lack of
competition.

For many centuries, the Christmas rose
was thought to possess powerful magical and
medicinal properties. In Greek mythology, it
was used by the physician Melampus to cure
the mad daughters of Proteus, god of the sea.
Because of this legend, the plant was often
used to treat the insane. Epictetus, a second
century Greek writer, said that the more
deluded a man was, the more hellebore he
would need. John Gerard, author of a 1597
herbal, wrote that hellebore was "good for
mad and furious men."

The hellebores gained such a reputation
for being magical that they were often used
to purify houses and drive out evil spirits.
The flower is often used as a symbol of
purity. According to legend, the Christmas
rose grew in the garden in heaven and was
tended by the angels, who called it the rose
of love. In Holland it is known as Christ's
herb, because it so often blooms at Christmas
time. An anonymous poem aptly describes
the character of this small flower:

> . . . this winter rose
> Blossoms amid the snows,
> A symbol of God's promise, care and
> love.

Perhaps the best-known legend about
the Christmas rose is of Madelon, a small
shepherd girl who came to Bethlehem on the
night that Christ was born. She had come to
see the miracle of his birth, but had no gift
for the Christ child. Sad and lonely, she
stood outside the manger and began to cry.
God looked down from heaven and saw her
tears and took pity on this small girl with
empty hands but a heart full of love. He sent
the angel Gabriel to her. Gabriel touched the
earth around her, and suddenly, through the
frozen ground, there appeared dozens of the
small white flowers that today we call
Christmas rose. Madelon happily picked an

armful of the blossoms and laid them at the manger.

The genus name, *Helleborus*, sheds a different light on the character of the little Christmas rose. The name is from two Greek words, *helein*, meaning "to kill," and *bora*, meaning "food." This name was given to the hellebores because the roots are poisonous. Even the bruised leaves give off a toxic substance, so handle the plant carefully. The species name *niger* was given because the root of this plant is black.

A closely related species is the Lenten rose, *H. orientalis*. It blooms somewhat later in the season, in March and April, and has blossom colors that range from green to white and many shades of pink and purple. It grows to a height of about 18 inches, and its cultural requirements are similar to those of the Christmas rose. Both the Christmas and the Lenten rose are native to limestone areas of Europe and Asia.

Sheila MacQueen, the *grande dame* of English flower arranging, considers the Christmas rose a "necessity for both garden and flower arrangers." She suggests that you force Christmas rose under a pane of glass to assure blossoms by Christmas. An arrangement of variegated holly, yellow jasmine, and flowers from the Christmas rose, she says, makes a perfect table arrangement for the holidays.

Both the Christmas and the Lenten rose will last longer indoors if their stems are conditioned when cut. Either hammer the ends of the stems or dip the ends into boiling water for thirty seconds, and then allow them to stand in deep water for 12 hours.

The seed heads are also attractive in arrangements. Pick them after the seeds have formed, and put them in a warm spot in water.

COMMON NAME:  Crocus
GENUS:  *Crocus*
SPECIES, HYBRIDS, CULTIVARS:
Blue: *C. biflorus, C. imperati, C. sieberi,*
*C. tomasinianus, C. versicolor;* yellow:
*C. aureus, C. chrysanthus,*
*C. korolkowii, C. sulphureus concolor,*
*C. susianus;* white: *C. fleischeri,*
*C. laevigatus, C. speciosus* (fall). Dutch
crocus cultivars—blue: Enchantress,
Pickwick, Queen of the Blues,
Remembrance, Striped Beauty; white: Jeanne
d'Arc, Peter Pan, Snowstorm; yellow: Golden
Yellow, Yellow Mammoth.
FAMILY:  Iridaceae
BLOOMS:  winter, spring, fall
TYPE:  perennial
DESCRIPTION:  A multitude of
crocuses are available today in colors ranging
from white to blue, purple, and yellow, and
with blooming seasons in late winter, early
spring, and autumn. The leaves are linear
and grasslike; the blossoms cup shaped and
proportionally large. Winter-blooming
varieties generally grow to a height of 3
inches. Spring- and fall-blooming species are
usually a bit taller, 4 to 5 inches.
CULTIVATION:  Crocuses grow from
corms, which should be planted 3 to 4
inches deep in early fall. Crocuses prefer soil
that is light, sandy, and not too rich, and
they will perform best in full sun or light
shade. Do not cut the leaves, but let them
die down naturally.

Crocuses are native to Spain, North Africa,
and Mediterranean regions and have been
known and used for centuries. According to
Claire Shaver Haughton's book *Green
Immigrants*, a jug decorated with crocuses
and dating back to 1500 B.C. was found in
Crete. *The English Gardener*, by Leonard
Maeger, reported a scroll from 1552 B.C.
listing the medicinal uses of crocus.

Because crocus has been well known
and loved by many civilizations, there are
many stories about the origin of the plant.
According to Greek mythology, Mercury
created the flower from Crocus, Europa's son
whom Mercury accidentally killed. In
another Greek legend Crocus was a youth
who fell in love with Smilax, who rejected
him. Crocus was distraught and begged the
gods to help him. The gods, taking pity on
him, changed him into the lovely crocus
plant. At this point, Crocus turned fickle, for
he won the love of Smilax but then rejected
her, and the gods turned her into a yew.

The oldest cultivated crocus is
*C. sativus*, which is the source of the herb
saffron. The Mongols are said to have carried
this plant to China. First record of crocus
coming to England was in the sixteenth
century when it arrived in the Elizabethan
court from the Mideast. It became quite
popular there and was mentioned by
Shakespeare, Francis Bacon, and the herbalist
John Gerard.

A dye made from the stigmas of crocus
was quite valuable, and golden cloth dyed
with crocus was worn by wealthy aristocrats
in both Europe and the Orient. King Henry
VIII of England outlawed sheets dyed with
saffron. His reasoning was that dyed sheets
were not washed as often as white ones, and
thus presented a health hazard.

The genus name, *Crocus*, is from the
Greek word *krokos*, which means "thread"
and refers to the stigmas (the tips of the
pistils on which pollen is deposited during
pollination), particularly those of the saffron
crocus. Saffron, which is collected from the
stigmas of *C. sativa*, has been, and still is,
quite a valuable product. In 1983 the price
of saffron was $4.59 for $1/40$ of an ounce.
This works out to be a little less than $3,000
per pound. It has been estimated, however,

that it takes over 4,000 crocus blossoms to make up an ounce of saffron.

In addition to being used as a cooking herb, saffron has also been used in perfumes, as medicine, and as a magical herb in certain religious rites. Many of the medicinal uses of saffron are somewhat questionable. Take, for example, the English custom of eating crocus seeds to help rheumatism—on the right side of the body only. If drunk in beer, saffron was thought to strengthen teeth. The Roman statesman and writer Pliny suggested that if saffron was worn around the neck, it would dispel the odors of wine and prevent drunkenness. Because the Greek poet Homer wrote that crocus was used to make the marriage bed of Zeus and Hera, Greeks used crocus petals to decorate their own marriage beds and to strew throughout banquet halls and in fountains.

Saffron tea is still listed in some herbals as being useful in breaking a fever and is sometimes recommended for treating measles victims.

According to the Victorian language of flowers, crocus was a symbol of youthful gladness. Crocus has also been considered a symbol of mirth, perhaps because of the superstition that crocus creates merriment and causes much laughter. Crocus was also thought to inspire love and was often sent between lovers.

An Austrian superstition held that it was unlucky to pick crocus blossoms because it would draw away your strength and make you weak.

COMMON NAME:  **cyclamen**
GENUS:  *Cyclamen*
SPECIES, HYBRIDS, CULTIVARS:
*C. purpurascens*—pink; blooms in fall.
*C. hederifolium*—vigorous, easy to grow.
*C. coum*—cultivated since 1596.
FAMILY:  Primulaceae
BLOOMS:  winter
TYPE:  perennial
DESCRIPTION:  Cyclamen has lovely pink-carmine-magenta nodding flowers, borne singly on stems that, on some species, coil downward. The foliage is also quite attractive, usually a dark, glossy green and sometimes mottled. With the necessary cultural conditions cyclamen can be used as a lovely ground cover. The plants reach a height of only 4 to 6 inches.
CULTIVATION:  Cyclamen is often grown indoors as a houseplant but is hardy in some southern areas and can be used effectively in rock gardens or in small clusters underneath trees and shrubs. The plants grow from corms, which should be planted 1 to 2 inches deep in late summer. They prefer rich, moist, shady areas. The corms do not multiply or divide so propagate by planting new corms or sowing seeds during the summer months. Be patient, though, for it may take as long as a year to get a bloom from seed.

Cyclamen was used as a medicinal herb long before it was known for its beauty. The bulbs contain a substance called cyclamin and are considered poisonous. Taken in small quantities, they can produce nervous tension and gastritis. In larger quantities, the symptoms become more severe, and cramps and paralysis can occur.

Roasting the corms destroys some of the toxicity, and they were sometimes beaten and made into small cakes. Eating these corms was thought to make one feel amorous and fall in love easily.

The medicinal uses of the plant were varied. An ancient English remedy suggested: "In case that a man's hair fall off, take this same wort, and put it into the nostrils." It was also widely used in childbirth. The powers of the plant were thought to be so great that it was considered very dangerous for a woman even to step on this plant while she was pregnant, for fear she would have the baby early.

———— *ঔ* ————

The genus name *Cyclamen* is from the Greek word *kyklos*, meaning "circle." Some say the name refers to the circular form of the corm; others say it is because of the spiral coil that the stalk makes after flowering. The common name sowbread comes from the fact that wild pigs grub for the roots. In some countries, the bulbs were at one time used for fodder.

COMMON NAME:  snowdrop
GENUS:  *Galanthus*
SPECIES, HYBRIDS, CULTIVARS:
*G. nivalis* 'Atkinsii'—blooms very early;
large flowers. *G.n.* 'Flore Pleno'—double
flowers. *G.n.* 'Lutescens'—yellow markings.
*G.n.* 'Simplex'—single flowers.
*G.n.* 'S. Arnott'—taller with fragrant large
flowers.
FAMILY:  Amaryllidaceae
BLOOMS:  winter
TYPE:  perennial
DESCRIPTION:  Snowdrops are tiny,
growing only to a height of 3 to 4 inches.
This allows them to be buried by late heavy
snows and survive with no hard feelings.
The flowers are small, white, and drooping.
CULTIVATION:  Plant snowdrop bulbs 3
to 4 inches deep in early fall. They prefer a
slightly shaded area with rich soil and plenty
of moisture. After they flower, lift them,
divide the bulbs, and replant them
immediately. Snowdrops look wonderful
naturalized in a woodland setting or at the
base of trees in the lawn, but remember that
they spread slowly.

The common name, snowdrop, refers to the
color of the flower and its resemblance to a
teardrop earring. The color of the flower is
also responsible for its genus name,
*Galanthus*, which is from the Greek word
for "milk flower." The species name *nivalis*
is also from Greek and means "near the
snow line." This is quite appropriate, for its
native habitat is alpine areas of Europe and
Asia.

Because it is a harbinger of spring and a
sign of returning life, snowdrop is considered
sacred and is a symbol of purity and chastity
in many European countries. It is considered
an herb of the Virgin Mary. In early spring
the image of Mary was removed from church
altars and snowdrop blossoms were scattered
in its place. Snowdrop has become the floral
symbol for the Feast of the Purification of
the Blessed Virgin on February 2, also
known as Candlemas Day. A poem from *An
Early Calendar of English Flowers* begins,
"The Snowdrop, in purest white arraie, First
rears her hedde on Candlemas daie."

In the Victorian language of flowers,
snowdrop is the symbol of hope and
consolation, and, it is the English floral
emblem for January.

In some English counties superstition
held that if you carried even a single blossom
of snowdrop, primrose, or violet into the
house when they first began to bloom, you
would have bad luck. Snowdrop in the house
has been called a death token. The reason?
English housewives said that the snowdrop
blossom looked like "a corpse in its shroud,
and that it always kept itself close to the
earth, seeming to belong more to the dead
than to the living."

The fact that snowdrop blooms so early
in the growing season has given rise to many
common names, including fair maid of
February, and *perce-neige*, French for
piercing the snow.

Snowdrop is marvelous for bringing
indoors in early spring (if you aren't
superstitious). Simply dig up a clump, enjoy
the blossoms indoors, and then replant it in
the garden when it is through blooming.

COMMON NAME: **winter jasmine**

GENUS: *Jasminum*

SPECIES, HYBRIDS, CULTIVARS:
*J. nudiflorum. J. polyanthum*—vigorous vine; grown indoors; sprays of white blossoms. *J. mesnyi*—primrose jasmine; evergreen vine with long, arching branches; lemon yellow flowers, February–April.
*J. officinale*—poet's jasmine; small, white, fragrant flowers in summer; not suitable in extremely cold climates; glossy, semi-evergreen leaves.

FAMILY: Oleaceae

BLOOMS: winter

TYPE: perennial

DESCRIPTION: Bright yellow flowers on some species of this vine brighten up the winter garden. It can also be grown as a shrub. The flowers are ³/₄ to 1 inch across and generally appear before the leaves, which are deciduous. The vines are graceful, green, and slender.

CULTIVATION: Winter jasmine needs full sun or partial shade but is adaptable to a wide range of conditions. It is considered hardy and easy to grow, and most species withstand cold particularly well. Selective pruning of dead branches will improve the health and appearance of the plant.

forbade even a leaf of it to leave his garden. One of his young gardeners disobeyed this order and presented his fiancée with a branch of this beautiful plant. Together they planted this branch and were able to raise many more plants from it. These they sold at a very high price, making a tidy sum to start housekeeping with. Since that time, Italian brides have worn a sprig of this jasmine on their wedding day as a token of good luck.

In the Victorian language of flowers, white jasmine means amiability.

Winter jasmine was introduced from China by English botanist Robert Fortune in 1844. It is the emblem of grace and elegance.

The Carolina jessamine, state flower for South Carolina, is not a true jasmine. The botanical name is *Gelsemium sempervirens*, and it is in the Loganiaceae family. It blooms from early to late spring and has a sweet fragrance. Carolina jasmine is extremely poisonous, and consuming any part of the plant is said to result in paralysis or even death. It was used as medicine during the nineteenth century but was dropped for this purpose when its extremely poisonous properties were discovered.

Of the 200 species of jasmines known, only about 15 are grown in gardens.

The white jasmine was introduced to England from India by Vasco da Gama in the sixteenth century. It was particularly cherished for its scent and was often used in perfumes. The Chinese name for this plant is *yeh-hsi-ming*, which is probably from the Persian name *ysmis*, meaning "white flower."

An Italian legend says that the first person to grow jasmine in Italy was the Duke Cosimo de Medici. The Duke was inordinately proud of this plant and jealously

# Appendix: Flowers in the Home

## Flower Arrangement

Julia Berrall, in her book *A History of Flower Arrangement*, says that "Ever since the early days of recorded history, when man was at last able to free himself from the necessities of the hunt and till the soil for his living instead, floral decoration has played an important part in his arts."

The fact that man has decorated with flowers since ancient times is indisputable. Ancient Egyptian pottery and jars include designs of flowers—particularly lotus, which was sacred to the goddess Isis, and mallow and corn poppy.

During the Golden Age of Greece, the use of flowers as decoration seemed to be limited to garlands and wreaths. The Greeks liked to use pleasantly scented plants, such as laurel and saffron. They were also partial to the rose, violet, lily, cornflower, iris, cyclamen, and crocus. Flowers were exchanged at many occasions, including weddings, the birth of a son, athletic events, and festivals.

Romans had a passion for roses, and they spread rose petals on their banquet tables and throughout their homes.

With the fall of Rome and the onset of the Dark Ages, the Church became increasingly powerful, and flowers were grown primarily for their medicinal and culinary value. The lily, however, was cherished for its beauty and its symbolism. Thought to be a flower sacred to the Virgin Mary, lilies were quite often included within religious art.

During the Renaissance, when flowers were once again grown for pleasure, floral arrangements were considered important decorations. Many paintings done in the late fifteenth and early sixteenth centuries depicted greatly detailed flower arrangements, including flowers such as the rose, lily, iris, violet, and columbine (often seven stalks of columbine were used to represent the seven gifts of the Holy Spirit).

By the seventeenth century, flower arranging became a favorite pastime of the wives of wealthy and prominent men. Social rules during this period forbade many activities, but arranging flowers was definitely socially acceptable. There were many rules and instructions on how to put together an arrangement, the most important of which was "love your flowers: by some subtle sense the dear things always detect their friends," as one writer put it.

It is ageless advice. Whether or not "the dear things" can actually detect your friendship, they will certainly respond better with tender loving care. Conditioning and care of the flowers you arrange is an indispensable step in creating a beautiful bouquet or arrangement.

## Conditioning the Flowers

By following certain rules and taking advantage of some tricks of the trade, you can condition your flowers to last longer in water.

The most important step is to choose good, healthy plant material. If a flower doesn't look good growing out in the garden, it is not going to look any better when you cut it and bring it indoors. During warm weather pick the flowers in early evening, when the plants have maximum food reserves and are full and turgid.

Try to maximize the amount of water the blossoms receive. To do this, cut stems at an angle and put them into water as soon as possible. You might want to carry a bucket of water to the garden so that as you cut, you can put the stems in water immediately.

Other general rules to follow are:

1. Avoid picking fully pollinated blossoms.
2. Recut stems underwater to prevent air pockets from forming in the stem.
3. Hollow-stemmed plants (such as delphiniums) last longer if the bottom of the stem is plugged with a bit of cotton.
4. Milky stems (found on poppies, dahlias, and many other plants) should be dipped into boiling water for thirty seconds, or the ends seared with a gas flame until they turn black.
5. Generally, use room-temperature water—never ice water.
6. Some plants respond well to a weak sugar solution (one tablespoon of sugar to one quart of water), a weak saline solution (one tablespoon of salt to one quart of water), or a weak starch solution.
7. Use clippers for cutting woody stems and flower scissors for softer stems.

## Drying Flowers

Many plants retain their shape and color quite well, and so they make good dried flowers. The easiest method for drying flowers is to hang them upside down in a dark, shady place and leave them at least a week. Bunch the flowers together according to type; pull off and discard the leaves. The flowers are hung upside down so the stems will be straight. Good air circulation is essential, so allow plenty of room between bunches. Hanging them up on hooks or wiring them to coat hangers are both good methods of hanging.

Flowers you intend to dry are best picked in mid-morning when the dew has evaporated but before the sun gets too hot. The following flowers are especially good for air drying.

allium
artemisia
baby's breath
clematis (seed heads)
columbine (seed heads)
delphinium
foxglove
globe amaranth
grape hyacinth (seed heads)
hollyhock
honesty (seed heads)
hosta (seed heads)
iris (seed heads)
lupine (seed heads)
poppy (seed heads)
scilla
statice
strawflower
yarrow (yellow)

## Pressed Flowers

Another good way to preserve flowers is to press them. Although elaborate flower presses are available, old telephone books and big catalogs will suffice. Flower presses do have an advantage: They usually contain blotting paper, which will help retain better color in the blossoms than newsprint will.

Flowers you choose to press should be thin and should have no thick or hard parts (although you can always remove the petals of flowers that have a hard center). Pick them when they are completely dry and are in prime condition.

Carefully place the flowers between pages of the book or layers of a plant press. Once the flowers have dried, they become quite brittle, so position them correctly before you close the book or screw down the top to the press. Flowers should be left to dry for one to three weeks, depending on the type of plant material you used. The thinner the individual petals, the less time necessary for drying.

Pressed flowers can be used to make stationery, wall hangings, or small framed pictures. Pressing flowers (common and

| Plant | Mordant | Color |
|---|---|---|
| black-eyed Susan | chrome | green shades |
| iris, purple | chrome | blue/violet |
| iris, yellow flag (root) | sulphate of iron | black |
| lily of the valley (leaves) | alum | green |
| marigold | alum | yellow |
| rose hips | alum | gray/rose |
| Saint John's wort | alcohol | yellow |
| Saint John's wort | vinegar | crimson |
| Saint John's wort | alum | greenish/yellow |
| zinnia | alum | yellow |

Other plants that make good dyes: anemone, calendula, chrysanthemum, coreopsis, crocus, daffodil, dahlia, daisy, African, geranium.

abundant flowers only) on a trip and using these to illustrate a travel book makes a beautiful and unique memento.

Although there are many methods of attaching pressed flowers to a background, one of the easiest is to use clear contact paper. Carefully arrange the flowers on the background as you wish, and then cover the entire area with contact paper.

The following flowers are some of the best to use for pressing.

alyssum, sweet
baby's breath
bachelor's button
calendula
Christmas rose
clematis
coreopsis (annual)
cosmos
daffodil (petals)
hollyhock
Johnny-jump-up
nicotiana
pansy
phlox
pink
primrose
poppy
violet

## Flowers for Dyeing

The flower garden provides an abundant supply of natural dyes. Leaves and flowers of many of our most beautiful flowers also are suitable for coloring wool or cotton. Good recipes and instructions for dyeing yarn and cloth are available in many books. Including mordants, such as chrome or alum, when you dye will not only fix the colors but will bring out sharper, brighter shades.

## Flowers for Cutting

**Artemisia:** dip stems in boiling water for twenty seconds; leave in warm water for two hours.

**Aster:** cut when 3/4 open and soak overnight in sugar solution. Lasts six to ten days.

**Bleeding heart:** dip stem ends into boiling water for ten seconds; leave in cool water three hours or more.

**Calla lily:** blossoms need no special treatment; leaves should be soaked in weak starch solution overnight.

**Campanula:** place stem ends in boiling water for twenty seconds; then plunge in deep, cool water for three hours or more.

**Chrysanthemum**:   cut in full bloom, remove lower foliage, hammer ends of stems, and place in water to their necks for three hours or more.

**Clematis**:   crush stem ends lightly and take lower leaves off; allow them a long drink before arranging.

**Coreopsis**:   cut blooms when fully open; place overnight in saline solution. Lasts seven to fourteen days.

**Cosmos**:   cut blooms when almost open; leave them in cool water overnight. Lasts five to eight days.

**Dahlia**:   dip stems in boiling water for twenty seconds; let stand in sugar solution plus one aspirin. Lasts five to seven days. Avoid using the larger blossoms, for they don't last as well as the smaller ones.

**Delphinium**:   cut blooms when tops are still in bud; fill stem with weak starch solution and plug end with a piece of cotton. Lasts seven days.

**Gaillardia**:   pick blooms when fully open; remove lower leaves and soak overnight in a weak sugar solution. Lasts seven days.

**Gladiolus**:   cut when buds begin to show color; set in cool water until ready to use. If placed in warm water, buds will open overnight. Lasts seven to ten days.

**Hosta, spring leaves**: dip stems in boiling water, submerge in cold water overnight. Flowers need no extra treatment. Lasts five days.

**Iris**:   give a long drink before arranging. Remove flowers as they fade. Lasts seven to ten days.

**Lily**:   handle gently, for they bruise easily. Cut stems on a slant; place in warm water for several hours. Lasts seven days.

**Marigold**:   scrape bottom of stem to expose inner tissue. Remove foliage beneath water level. Lasts seven days.

**Narcissus**:   cut as buds show color; wipe off sap before putting stems in water. Arrange in shallow water. Lasts seven days.

**Phlox**:   cut when clusters are half open; split stems and soak overnight in cool water.

**Pink, carnation**:   cut stems at an angle between joints and put in water immediately. Cut when centers are tight and outer petals are firm. Lasts ten to fourteen days.

**Peony**:   cut when petals begin to open; put in warm water. Lasts seven days.

**Poppy**:   cut before fully open. Dip stems in boiling water for twenty seconds; place in cool water for several hours.

**Primrose**:   lasts four days. Prick stems just under flower head; plunge into warm water for several hours.

**Rose**:   cut as buds begin to open; hammer stems. Lasts five to ten days.

**Sweet pea**:   handle as little as possible. Arrange in shallow water. Lasts seven days.

**Tulip**:   cut off white part of stem. Wrap stems together in bunches in newspaper; place in a warm, weak starch solution. Prick stems just under flower head with a pin.

**Vinca**:   either burn ends or dip in boiling water. Place in cool water overnight.

**Zinnia**:   cut right above a leaf joint; remove extra foliage; place ends in boiling water for twenty seconds and then place in warm water for several hours.

## Garden Flowers for Food and Medicine

Ever since the first cave dweller got the first stomach ache, people have looked toward plants to relieve their aches and pains. Which plants would cure which ailments? The question is ageless. Answers first came from (probably often painful) trial and error. Eventually, though, this was backed by experience and knowledge passed down from one generation to another. Different civilizations, even though they were separated by time and great distances, used similar plants to cure the same ills.

People in primitive societies believed, and still believe today, that sickness was a punishment from the gods. They assumed that their discomfort was a direct consequence of their actions. In these societies, no one knew why plants were able to cure many ailments. The men and women who were knowledgeable about plants and able to treat various illnesses with their herbs were held in special esteem and took an honored place in the social order. Perhaps some of this distinction was based on fear, for the plants could harm as well as heal. An angry herbalist could do great harm.

Because superstition was a strong factor in the cures they obtained, herbalists included many rites and rituals along with their magical herbs.

One of the first writers to address the field of plants and medicine was Dioscorides, a Roman who published *De Materia Medica* around A.D. 60. He was a contemporary of Pliny, who wrote *Naturalis Historia*, a work much admired and used by both ancient and medieval peoples.

During the Dark Ages and Middle Ages monks were the primary instruments for keeping alive the medical and herbal writings of the Greeks and Romans. Outside the cloister, herb men and women, bone setters, and healers prevailed, and superstition and folklore reigned.

During the years A.D. 400 to 1500, the Church had great power. Since Christians believed that illnesses were caused by sin, they also believed that the greatest cures were obtained through prayer and repentance. It was, however, part of a monk's duty to care for the sick, and these men were able to use many of the herbs growing in their own gardens.

Monks during the medieval period were in a very good position to perpetuate the teachings of the Greeks and Romans. Not only were they excellent copyists, able to transcribe the classical writings, they were also wonderful gardeners, for they had the time and opportunity to learn a great deal about the herbs while working in the cloister gardens. Communication between monasteries allowed for an exchange of information about plants as well as religious matters.

The first herbal published in English was written by a monk, John of Gaddesden, between 1314 and 1317. Entitled *Rosa Medicinae*, it combined Greek, Arabic, Jewish and Saxon writings about plants and medicine.

In the mid-sixteenth century an Italian physician proposed the doctrine of signatures, a method for choosing medicinal plants. Giambattista Porta suggested that the "creator had marked out a path for mankind in treatment of disease and injury by placing a sign or hint on plants which would be useful in healing them." In other words, whatever a plant physically resembled, that is what it would cure. For example, plants covered with hairs were used to treat baldness or to wash and clean hair. The overlapping scales of lily bulbs were used to treat scaly skin. The bright red sap of bloodroot was used to treat blood disorders, and the liver-shaped leaf of hepatica was used to treat problems of the liver.

This simple method of selecting the right plant for various ailments became quite popular, and a phytognomonica (a book of plant indicators) was published explaining the different plant signs. Science and magic, truth and superstition competed to dominate the minds and souls of men until the seventeenth century.

In the late 1500s an Englishman, John Gerard, published his *Herball or Generall Historie of Plantes*. For centuries it was prized for the mass of information it contained, and even today it is popular, in spite of its blatant errors and inconsistencies.

The use of garden flowers in natural remedies enjoyed great popularity during the 1930s. An English physician, Dr. Edward, Bach, was one of the first "holistic healers" treating the body as a whole and not simply dealing with the separate parts. His book *The Bach Flower Remedies* includes recipes and instructions for using thirty-eight different flowers. Each flower was used to treat a different emotion that, Dr. Bach felt, could cause disease. Oils from flowers were extracted, mixed with water, and preserved with brandy. Two or three drops of this mixture were drunk several times during the day.

For example, pink impatiens was thought to be useful to those suffering irritability, gentian was good for those who were easily discouraged, and clematis was for those who were oversensitive.

The use of plants as medicines and folk remedies gradually lost favor. As man became more sophisticated, he came to rely on synthetic drugs and became more and more removed from natural remedies. Today, however, some suspect that the very purity of laboratory-made drugs may cause harmful side effects within the patient. Perhaps many of the plants used for medicines contain "checks and balances" that prevent some of these side effects.

Modern medicine is beginning to take another long look at the folk remedies that have been used for centuries. Many of the herbal remedies have proven to be effective, and scientists today are learning a great deal from the still-existing herb healers. The World Health Organization has created a Collaborating Center for Traditional Medicine at the University of Illinois to learn from these healers. Approximately four billion people, most in the Third World, still depend on traditional medicine for their primary health care. The World Health Organization's center hopes that in these countries where "modern medicine" has not intruded, solutions to many health-care needs can be obtained from the plants that grow there naturally. This provides a powerful incentive for strong conservation practices. Though some plants have been used for centuries for healing purposes, scientists throughout the world have just begun to discover the treasures contained within our native flora. To lose even one plant species might mean the loss of ingredients that could prove to be essential to our survival.

## Ancient herbal remedies

Arthritis: violet
Blood circulation: marigold
Bronchitis: primrose
Colic: verbena
Complexion: rose water, corn poppy
Coughs and convulsions: iris
Cuts and wounds: yarrow
Epilepsy: peony
Eye disease: cornflower, marigold
Gout: mallow
Head lice: larkspur
Heartburn: yarrow
Heart disease: foxglove, carnation
Infertility: wallflower
Influenza: pansy

Intestinal disorders: vinca
Jaundice: wallflower
Liver disorders: daisy
Nosebleeds: yarrow
Poisoning: columbine
Rheumatism: saffron crocus
Stomach aches: verbena
Sunburn: iris
Vertigo: primrose
Whooping cough: poppy

## Edible Garden Flowers

In addition to their medicinal value, plants and flowers have also been indispensable throughout the ages for seasoning food. Many of the plants we grow in our gardens today for their beauty were at one time grown for their flavor. Many are still useful. Be creative, but be sure you know the identity of the plants you work with. Remember that some of our favorite garden plants are poisonous and should not be taken internally.

Gather plant material in early morning before the sun gets on it. Wash it gently, pull off the petals, and blot them dry. Store them in a plastic bag in the refrigerator.

**To make syrup:**   Place the desired amount of petals in one cup of water. Boil one to three minutes. Strain through cheesecloth and add two cups of sugar. Boil this mixture ten minutes, or until syrup forms. Do not overcook.

**To flavor honey:**   Add the desired amount of finely chopped leaves or petals to a jar of mild honey. Place the jar in a warm-water bath and boil gently for thirty minutes. Cool and store for several days before using. This can be strained or used unstrained.

**To flavor vinegar:**   Chop fresh petals or leaves, or used dried ones. Pour room-temperature vinegar over the plant material and let it stand one week. Strain and store the vinegar in a cool place.

**To flavor stock (vegetable or meat):**   Simmer stock with fresh or dried leaves or petals. The longer you simmer, the stronger the herb flavor.

**To flavor butter:**   Place chopped petals in between layers of softened butter. Refrigerate at least one week before using.

**To pickle flowers:**   Place layers of buds or flowers in a glass or ceramic bowl, putting sugar between each layer. Pour boiling vinegar (cider or white) over the layers, add a piece of mace, and store for one week before using.

**To make jam or jelly:**   Chop petals and add them to water. Boil gently to extract color and flavor. The length of time you boil this depends on the plant material used. Strain and measure the resulting liquid. For every cup of liquid used, add one cup of sugar. Boil this mixture until the jelly stage is reached (a drop of the liquid should form a ball in cold water). Sure-jell can be used if desired. Pour into hot jelly jars and refrigerate or seal properly.

**To make tea:**   Use two to three teaspoons of dried (or sometimes fresh) leaves or petals for every cup of water. Steep the plant material in boiling water for three to ten minutes, depending on the type of plant material and personal preference.

**To make flower fritters:**   Chop up flowers into the fritter batter. Fry the fritters as you would pancakes.

The following flowers are considered edible. Their flavors vary from quite sweet to hot and spicy. Experiment with different blossoms and leaves in your favorite recipes. Most of these will add an exotic flavor and extra color to any dish. Use large open flowers such as hollyhocks, tulips, and day lilies to hold a dip for a party. Use smaller flowers such as Johnny-jump-ups or violets to make candies. Be sure of the identification of each of these before you eat it.

chrysanthemum
day lily
geranium
gladiolus
hollyhock
jasmine (not the Carolina jessamine,
   which is poisonous)
Johnny-jump-up

nasturtium
pansy
peony
poppy
rose
sunflower
tulip
violet

# SELECTED BIBLIOGRAPHY

Anderson, Frank J. *Cultivated Flowers*. New York: Abbeville Press Publishers, 1981.

Bach, Edward, and F.J. Wheeler, M.D. *The Bach Flower Remedies*. New Canaan, Conn.: Keats Publishing, 1952.

Bianchini, Francesco, and F. Corbetta. *Health Plants of the World: Atlas of Medicinal Plants*. New York: Newsweek Books, 1975.

Boland, Bridget, and Maureen Boland. *Old Wives' Lore for Gardeners*. New York: The Bodley Head, 1976.

Brown, Dennis A. (editor). *Gardening for All*. Secaucus, N.J.: Chartwell Books, 1977.

Brown, James, and Louise Bush. *America's Garden Book*. New York: Charles Scribner's Sons, 1980.

Calkins, Carroll C. (editor). *Reader's Digest Illustrated Guide to Gardening*. Pleasantville, New York: Reader's Digest Books, 1978.

Coats, Alice M. *Flowers and Their Histories*. New York: McGraw Hill Book Company, 1968.

Coats, Peter. *Flowers in History*. New York: Viking Press, 1970.

Conway, David. *The Magic of Herbs*. New York: E.P. Dutton and Company, 1973.

Diamond, Denise. *Living with Flowers*. New York: William Morrow and Company, 1982.

Dobelis, Inge N. (editor). *Magic and Medicine of Plants*. Pleasantville, N.Y.: Reader's Digest Books, 1986.

Drew, John K. *Pictorial Guide to Hardy Perennials*. Kalamazoo, Mich.: Merchants Publishing Company, 1984.

Durant, Mary. *Who Named the Daisy? Who Named the Rose?* New York: Congdon & Weed, 1983.

Ewart, Neil. *The Lore of Flowers*. New York: Sterling Publishers, 1982.

Fiore, Evelyn, and Josephine von Miklos. *Gardener's World*. New York: Ridge Press Books, Random House, 1968.

Friend, Hilderic. *Flower Lore*. Rockport, Mass.: Para Research, 1981.

Gordon, Lesley. *The Mystery and Magic of Trees and Flowers*. Devon, Great Britain: Webb and Bower, 1985.

Grace, Princess, of Monaco. *My Book of Flowers*. Garden City, N.Y.: Doubleday and Company, 1980.

Greenaway, Kate. *The Illuminated Language of Flowers*. London: G. Routledge, 1978 (reprint of 1884 edition).

Haughton, Claire Shaver. *Green Immigrants: The Plants That Transformed America*. New York: Harcourt, Brace, Jovanovich, 1978.

Healey, B.J. *A Gardener's Guide to Plant Names*. New York: Charles Scribner's Sons, 1972.

Hollingsworth, Buckner. *Flower Chronicles*. Rahway, N.J.: Rutgers University Press, 1958.

Jacob, Dorothy. *A Witch's Guide to Gardening*. New York: Taplinger Publishing Company, 1964.

Kerr, Jessica. *Shakespeare's Flowers*. New York: Crowell Junior Books, 1969.

L.H. Bailey Hortorium, Cornell University. *Hortus Third*. New York: Arco Publishing Company, 1977.

Le Strange, Richard. *A History of Herbal Plants*. New York: Arco Publishing Company, 1977.

Martin, Laura C. *Wildflower Folklore*. Chester, Conn.: The Globe Pequot Press, 1986.

Martin, Laura C. *The Wildflower Meadow Book*. Chester, Conn.: The Globe Pequot Press, 1984.

Mercatante, Anthony S. *The Magic Garden*. New York: Harper and Row, 1976.

Page, Robin. *Cures and Remedies the Country Way*. New York: Summit Books, 1978.

Powell, Claire. *The Meaning of Flowers*. Boulder, Colorado: Shambhala Publications, n.d.

Rohde, Eleanour Sinclair. *Rose Recipes from Olden Times*. New York: Dover Publications, 1973.

Sackville-West, V. *Garden Book*. London: Shuckburgh Reynolds, 1986.

Shosteck, Robert. *Flowers and Plants*. New York: The New York Times Book Company, 1974.

Thomson, William A.R. (editor). *Medicines from the Earth: A Guide to Healing Plants*. San Francisco: Harper and Row, 1978.

# INDEX